GW01091082

# FINDING *your* CLOVER

## AFTER a LOSS

BY J. DAWN ROUNTREE

ILLUSTRATIONS BY PIPPA MCNAY

Finding Your Clover After A Loss

Copyright © 2014 by J. Dawn Rountree

No part of this book may be reproduced or transmitted in any form or by
any means electronic or mechanical, including photocopying or by any
information storage without permission in writing from the copyright
owner.

If you would like to do any of the above, please contact
jdawn@tootlevillepublishing.com

Cover design, book design and layout by Jim L. Friesen

Library of Congress Control Number: 2014911687

International Standard Book Number: 978-0-9904722-0-9

Printed in the United States of America by Mennonite Press, Inc., Newton,
KS, www.mennonitepress.com

# Prologue

On June 23, 2000, my life changed forever. That was the day that my husband Ralph was diagnosed with kidney cancer. When our doctor said the dreaded word cancer, we both felt as if the wind had been knocked out of us. Even though many of my family members had died of cancer, cancer was a rarity in my husband Ralph's family, something we never thought would happen to him.

Surgery was scheduled for July 13. Since we had a few weeks until surgery, we decided to make a trip to Colorado, to retrace some of our favorite haunts in the mountains, to visit with friends, not knowing if he would live through the surgery when we returned to Kansas.

Fortunately, he did survive the surgery, and an enormous cancer and his left kidney were removed. But within a year, the cancer began to grow again, and a second surgery was not an option. Realizing how precious time was, we made a conscious decision to live each day as fully as possible. We spent time with family, made memories and photographs, and my husband lived to see two more grandchildren born.

The first five years after his diagnosis were fairly good, but August 2, 2005, he became bedfast when the cancer spread throughout his body. It was difficult to watch one of the most independent, full-of-life people I had ever known become totally dependent, but we were thankful for every day we had together.

Ralph died on February 28, 2006. On that day, my grief walk began in earnest. I felt as if three-fourths of me was gone, and my heart ached for him. I visited the cemetery almost every day—that was where I could feel closest to him even though I knew he was no longer there.

One spring day I took a walk around the cemetery and noticed the dates on the markers of several couples I had known before their passing. One thing stood out! I noticed that, for several of the couples, it was only a year or two from the time that one died until the other one died.

I wondered how much the loss of their spouse had impacted the second person who had died not long after the first. I wondered if the one who was left had grieved himself/herself to death.

That day was my turning point—my wakeup call. I did some self-talk and told myself, "You are only 64 years old, so you need to get on with it." Even though I still felt like my heart was breaking, I realized I needed to do whatever I could to survive. I recognized that there must be some reason, some purpose for me to be alive.

Shortly after that cemetery walk, a friend suggested that I start writing my thoughts, and I did. I had small notebooks in the kitchen, by my bedside, and in the car. I found that writing helped ease the pain of my loss.

About a year after my husband's death, I began leading a bereavement group for a hospice program, and each month I wrote an article related to grief for the group members. The idea for turning the articles into a book came to me when my present husband Tom and I drove to Alaska in 2009 with some of my sisters and their husbands.

That is when I wrote "The Story of Little Bear," the first story in this book. When we saw that little black bear beside the road in his clover patch, his coat shining in the sun, it was obvious that Little Bear was content. He was happy. Springtime had come, and life was good. He had found his patch of clover!

By then my life had already changed drastically. A couple of years after Ralph died, I remarried. Even though my life was totally different, I had found contentment in my life with Tom. But I still had an urge to make something good come from my forty-four years with Ralph. I felt I could do this by passing along some of my stories to others who are grieving—thus my motivation for *Finding Your Clover after a Loss*.

Life can be good again after a loss. Even though you will be forever changed and life will be different, life can be good. If you move forward, you will never forget the one who died. I certainly have not.

So *Don't Waste Your Sorrows*, as the title of a book by Paul Billheimer says. Your loved one would want you to be happy. Search for ways to rebuild your life and turn your loss into something good, your very own clover, whatever that might be.

# Dedication

*This book is dedicated to the life and memory
of four special women.*

*To Debra Kay Pyle, Clay Center, Kansas, born
September 17, 1953, and died March 5, 2013.
She was my friend and my encourager,
as she was for so many.*

*To my beautiful Aunt Helene,
born October 22, 1926, Santa Fe, Tennessee,
and died June 16, 2013.
She always had encouraging words for all
her nieces and nephews.*

*To Mary Youngblood Kuyper, born Galena,
Missouri, January 18, 1941. She was my
dear friend for forty-eight years, from 1966 to
February 13, 2014, the day of her death. She was
a well-known columnist for a newspaper in the
Ozarks, an inspiration to many.*

*To my little sister Gay Celeste Corlew, Dover,
Tennessee, my special encourager.*

*I have been blessed with the presence of these
special ladies in my life.*

# Table of Contents

# Introduction

*Finding Your Clover Patch*

As a very young child I remember sitting in patches of white clover blossoms with my older sister Joy in the springtime. We picked the white blooms, leaving the stems long enough to tie around the clover blossoms. We strung the clovers into necklaces, bracelets, or rings. Then we proudly wore our new "jewelry," feeling elegant and beautiful!

Other times my siblings and I would sit in a clover patch, carefully, patiently searching for a four-leaf clover—that symbol of good luck. If we were fortunate enough to find one, we preserved our newly found treasure by pressing it in a book or Bible. (I have recently found that the leaves of four-leaf clovers stand for faith, hope, love, and luck.)

When we lived on the farm when I was a child, my dad grew patches of crimson clover. The deep-red blossoms created a beautiful site! In my later years as an adult, I remember seeing field after field of yellow clover in Nebraska, blooming in profusion, breathtaking sites in the sunlight, and a haven for busy bees gathering nectar for honey! So it is no wonder I was thrilled when I saw a little black bear munching yellow clover beside the highway in 2009. He had found his clover patch, and he was content!

After the death of my husband Ralph in 2006, it was difficult to believe that life could ever be good again. My dream of retiring with him was gone, and I was unsure where to turn or what to do. Then little by little, I became hopeful as my heart began to heal.

I would have never dreamed how much my life would change after Ralph's death. I had decided I would probably never remarry, but I married Tom. I never dreamed I would ever sell my place in the country called Thornberry Acres which I loved, but I did. I never thought I could be content living in town instead of the country, but I am. I also changed jobs and began writing. So my new "clover patch" was nothing like I would have imagined.

In nature there are many varieties of clovers—three-leafed, four-leafed, five-leafed, and clovers of many colors—red, lavender, white, yellow, and pink, just to name a few.

Just as different kinds of clover add beauty to fields and provide nectar for bees, life holds new opportunities just waiting to be discovered. I wish you faith, hope, love, and luck as you search for your own contentment, your own clover patch, as you make this world a better place for yourself and others as a result of your loss.

# Acknowledgements

It would be impossible to name all who have impacted my life, resulting in this book. I would not be writing about grief if my first husband of forty-four years, Ralph Timothy Thorn, had not died. He encouraged me to try things I would have never dreamed possible.

A special thank you to my present husband Tom who encourages me as I write. He is patient with my many hours at the computer and is a wonderful husband.

A thank you to my family—my children, my sisters and brother, and aunts and uncles.

Others I would like to thank include Kendra Worthen who allowed me to write for hospice; the hospital staff; my Meadowlark Hospice co-workers and bereavement group members; the staff and readers of my hometown newspaper, the *Miltonvale Record*; my many friends.

A special thanks to Lilly Hitsman for her invaluable editing skills and to Pippa McNay for her beautiful artwork. Lilly and Pippa, I believe our paths were supposed to cross!

Without the guidance and expertise of Judy Entz, consultant, and Jim Friesen, designer, at Mennonite Press, this book would not have been published—you guided me well!

Last, a special thank you to Mr. Sheldon Harnick, lyricist, for allowing me to use his beautiful words from "Sunrise, Sunset" in the final chapter of this book.

# The Story of Little Bear

*d*uring our trip to Alaska in the summer of 2009, one of my goals was to see a bear—a black bear, brown bear, any kind of bear. While traveling through British Columbia, Canada, we did, to my delight, see a bear! The bear was not very large, but his black fur shone in the bright sunlight, literally glistening against a backdrop of spring-green grass intermingled with lush patches of yellow clover beside the highway.

What a sight! My husband Tom pulled the car over, joining others who had already stopped to soak in the view. Camera shutters were clicking. At first, the little black bear stood as he munched the green grass and clover. *Bite, bite, munch, munch. Bite, bite, munch, munch.*

After a bit, the little bear seemed to tire from standing up, and as we continued to watch, Little Bear sat down on his bottom. He continued to eat the juicy grass and clover, bobbing his head down to the ground for each new bite. *Bite, bite, munch, munch. Bite, bite, munch, munch.* Little Bear seemed oblivious to his large group of spectators—he was enjoying life!

*Then* Little Bear laid down in the grass, paws in front of him, tummy on the ground, and continued his breakfast of grass and clover from a closer vantage point. *Bite, bite, munch, munch.* He had found his clover, wonderful delicious clover. He still paid no attention to the spectators gawking at him. He was in his clover patch. Life was good—Little Bear was content.

After some minutes, we reluctantly left the sight to travel onward toward Alaska, our final destination on the trip. When we left, Little Bear was still flat-down in the clover patch, breaking off bites of breakfast with his teeth. *Bite, bite, munch, munch.*

The lesson from Little Bear hit me! He had found his place in the sun, and nothing seemed to be worrying him on that sunny morning. He truly had found a place of peace, of enjoyment, unmindful of the audience gazing at him. Life was simple, but good. *Ahh, contentment.*

In our lives, we may find ourselves chasing an illusive dream as we travel toward our final destination. We may search for contentment and happiness in relationships, in jobs, and in the acquisition of things as we travel along the Road of Life. We may search for money, prestige, fortune or fame—search for something to fill the voids or holes in our lives.

Sometimes we forget about our Creator and the simple things in life that can bring us real contentment—a new friend, a walk on a cool day, or the smile of a grandchild. Wild flowers growing by the road may take on a new wonder if you take the time to look at the delicacy of their design. How about the song of a mockingbird, holding hands with someone you love, spending time with family?

If you have experienced the loss of a loved one, the "hole" in your heart may seem like a cavern. You may long for the life that you used to have with the one you loved, and your heart may ache, almost physically. You may be challenged to find your own new patch of clover.

Your "clover patch" may be in a different location, or you may find red clover in place of the yellow clover you used to have. Even though your clover patch may change, life must go on as you move on to a new and different contentment.

If you take the time to look, you may find your clover patch right under your nose! Or you may have to search a little! It only costs a little time to pause, to enjoy life along the way—to take life in slowly—*bite, bite, munch, munch. Contentment!*

*"Surely there is something in the unruffled*
*calm of nature that overawes our little anxieties*
*and doubts; the sight of the deep-blue sky and*
*the clustering stars above seem to impart*
*a quiet to the mind."*
—Jonathan Edwards

# Conversation
# with Cows

*N*umber Twenty-Seven and Number Forty-Eight trotted toward me and reached the fence before the rest of the herd. I greeted them at the end of the pasture with "How are you, babies?" They were two very inquisitive Holsteins, black-and-white cows that lived on the other side of the fence in a pasture west of my acreage.

I had a routine. Some days after getting off work, I headed toward the Walking Path. Walking was my salvation—it helped me fight depression after the death of my husband the last day of February of that year. His death left a gaping hole in my heart. The house no longer held his laughter. There was no one to welcome me home; no one to talk to, no one to eat with. So I avoided the loneliness of the house by walking the path.

After winter lost its grip and warmer weather replaced the cold chill of winter, the spring grass emerged. For years my husband and I had kept a walking path cut around the pasture. But with the arrival of the spring grass, I also cut a new area at the west end of the pasture, an area large enough for an outdoor seat so I could watch the sun set. I then bought a glider seat and placed it in my newly-mowed space. I named my special place Peaceful Place—a name that described it well.

At Peaceful Place, I could enjoy the evening breeze and watch the sun go down. Some evenings the sunsets were glorious as the pinks, golds, and oranges painted the west-ern sky! My husband had told me, "Remember me when you see the sunset," and each time I saw a beautiful sunset, my thoughts were of him. How could I ever forget him?

Besides the sunset, there was something else special about Peaceful Place—the cows! There were close to twenty cows who were excited to see me. No matter how far from the fence they were, when they saw me walking the path, here they came—some faster than others, hurrying toward me. They inquisitively listened as I greeted them.

Each cow had a numbered ear tag, and I soon learned to watch for #27 and #48 which usually led the pack—they were the most curious! They came up close to the fence and dangled their heads over. Their big kind brown eyes watched me while I watched them. And I had my "conversations with cows."

I appreciated those black-and-white Holsteins because they gave me a diversion from my loneliness. Friends and family still cared. They had attended the funeral, sent cards and memorials and still called from time to time. But they had returned to their normal routines—they had grieved and moved on. But I, like so many others experiencing a loss, was left to face each day without my husband, and the cows became my buddies.

It was up to me to figure out how to cope, how to grieve, and how to rebuild my life. But I would never have guessed that cows would have helped! I am sure they did not understand a single word I said, but they came. They were there!

As you walk your Path of Grief, hopefully you will find a friend or family member to accompany you on your path. And perhaps you will find your own Peaceful Place, wherever that may be. Even if your path is lonely, keep walking, one day at a time, one foot in front of the other. If you stumble, get back up, but keep walking. With the passage of time, each day will become a bit easier. Hang on, and just keep walking.

*"Grief is not a sign of weakness, nor a lack of faith. It is the price of love."*
—Author unknown

# All New
# Batteries

When Will Thomas, our youngest grandson, was almost four years old, my husband Tom and I took care of him on Tuesdays while his mother attended school. He was, and still is, "all boy," brown-eyed, with light brown hair. He is inquisitive, and "his wheels are always turning." One day while he was with us, he and I went by the funeral home where my husband was the funeral director at the time.

There was a ninety-three-year-old lady in a casket in the funeral home on that particular day. Will had never seen anyone in a casket before that day. First, Will said, "I want to get closer," and he and I moved closer to the lady.

Then he said, "She's asleep."

Then I replied, "No, she is not asleep. She died."

Will then asked Tom to lift him up, stating that he wanted "to see her better," and Tom complied with Will's request.

Will Thomas again declared, "She's asleep." He then asked, "When is she going to wake up?"

I explained simply that she had died, that "her body was old," "that her body was broken," that "her body would no longer work," appropriate explanations, I thought, for a child his age. I told him that she had "gone to heaven," but her body would have to be buried.

Tom and I could tell that Will Thomas was still struggling with the new concept. Developmentally, at almost four, children think that a person will wake up and resume activities as before. Will Thomas took some moments to further think about what Tom and I had told him and then confidently proclaimed, *"We can get her some new batteries!"*

Then Tom and I patiently explained that "new batteries" for this lady would not make her body work again, but we privately chuckled at Will Thomas' solution to the problem—*"new batteries."* But the conversation also made me think about the "the big picture"—life, death, and beyond.

If someone you love has fought a life-threatening illness, in a sense, you and your doctor may have looked for the "new batteries" to keep your loved one alive. Perhaps you fought with everything in you, looking, searching for a cure, a treatment, as my first husband Ralph and I did when he was battling kidney cancer.

And sometimes batteries may physically help prolong a person's life, for instance, when a pacemaker is implanted to help a person's ailing heart. But when all treatments fail and there are no longer options, try as we may, we cannot keep our loved one with us on this side. Then, for us, the excruciating pain begins!

Looking backwards thousands of years, many cultures and religions believe that this life is temporary, that there is something far better for us on the other side. The ancient Egyptians strongly believed death is just a continuation of life, so much so that they built the Great Pyramids and stocked them with food, clothing, boats, and treasures to assist their departed loved ones on their journeys into the afterlife.

Many in the United States also believe that death is just a continuation of life on the other side. Many of us believe, in a sense, we will get *"all new batteries"*—that those who could not walk will have the ability to run, jump and dance. We believe that we will no longer be old, that those who could no longer speak will be able to speak and to sing! That those who were in pain will no longer hurt—reassuring thoughts that our loved ones are in a better place and are physically well.

But sometimes, for those who are grieving, the reminder that our loved one is in a better place may not provide the intended comfort. Yes, it is wonderful for the one on the other side. But the griever may have a gaping hole in his heart, an aching to be with the one they loved!

And the reminder of the good fortune of the one who has gone on probably will not fix a broken heart or take away the longing. But then slowly, ever so slowly, the pain will become a little less severe as the healing process begins. Grieving hurts! But hurting does not mean you are weak—it means you loved someone dearly. That is the price you pay for loving. So hang on—it does easier.

*"Is death the last sleep? No—it is the last and final awakening."*
—Sir Walter Scott

# Castles in the Sand

*T*he sand castle stood erect, proud, and precisely built with symmetrically placed round towers, fashioned from wet sand. I could imagine the builders packing buckets with the wet sand, then turning them upside-down, gingerly removing the containers to expose each new tower!

The castle complex itself was large, sprawling, and surrounded by a moat that was filled with water from the Gulf. From the looks of the castle, the builders must have planned for their building adventure before arriving at the beach. They must have gathered cans, plastic dishes, and buckets for their excursion with the hope of building a masterpiece.

My husband Tom and I came upon the sand castle work-of-art in 2010 on the coast of Biloxi, Mississippi, after Hurricane Katrina had pummeled the coastline in 2005, ripping out trees, washing away the sand, and destroying buildings. White sand had been hauled back to the beach, and some of the damage had been repaired, whereas many lots still lay bare and forsaken.

As we looked at the sand castle, we assumed the builders were children, giggling as they built, but maybe the castle builders were adults just having fun in the warm spring weather. But regardless of *who* the builders were, there was probably chatter as the architects discussed *how* to build their castle.

Perhaps, when they were finished, they stepped back

from their creation to survey their work, thinking "That's pretty good!" And it was good—a piece of work to admire!

But there was one major problem. The elaborate sand castle was built close to the edge of the water while the tide was out. More than likely, the builders were aware that their handiwork would be washed away when the tide came back in.

So was it worth all the time and effort to build a structure that would only stand for a few hours? It must have been. Maybe the fun was in "the building," enjoying the moment, even though they probably knew the tide would soon wash away their project. Perhaps it was more important for the eager builders to enjoy their building experience rather than the final product, the sand castle.

As my husband Tom and I continued our stroll on the beach that day, we observed the meandering coastline that was once lined with buildings before Katrina. Now the landscape was only intermittently dotted with structures. Some parking lots still lay vacant, and only the foundations of some businesses remained.

Hurricane Katrina is usually best remembered for the destruction of New Orleans, but the 450-mile-wide hurricane also stretched along the Mississippi coast which included Bixoli-Gulfport, Mississippi, bearing 80-85 mile-per-hour winds. Her force wreaked havoc on homes, businesses, historical sites, and the ships in the harbor.

Water from flooding reached 20 feet, and two-story buildings were assaulted by ships that acted as battering rams, banging into the second stories. Beauvoir, the home of Jefferson Davis, the southern president elected during the Civil War, was partially spared, but porches were never rebuilt to their original design, and the Jefferson Davis Museum was largely destroyed.

Many restaurants and businesses were gone forever.

The losses had just been too great for the owners to rebuild. Perhaps they were financially wiped out, or maybe they were afraid to build again, afraid another storm would again wash away their investment and hard work.

Our walk on the beach reminded me of a song called "Anyway" by Martina McBride. The lyrics to her song talk about how one storm can wash away everything that a person has built, but we should "build it anyway." There is truth in the song—natural disasters such as earthquakes, tornadoes, hurricanes, and floods can devastate property and lives in an instant.

An accident or a major illness can wreak havoc on lives, emotionally and financially, taking away hopes and dreams. When someone we love dies, our worlds are turned upside down. We may wonder which direction to go and may lose our motivation to try to rebuild our lives. Our "sand castles," so to speak, have been washed out to sea.

Major losses can cause us to quit dreaming, planning, and building, so it may take every ounce of courage we can muster to keep on going. If you are facing some difficult circumstances, you may have to make a choice—whether to just exist or try to rebuild your life. So take a deep breath and muster your courage. Then with the help of God and others, try again—rebuild your sand castle and enjoy the journey.

*"You can never cross the ocean unless you have the courage to lose sight of the shore."*
—Christopher Columbus

# Those Kite-Eating Trees

*C*harlie Brown is one of the original characters in Charles Schultz's *Peanuts* comic strip which began in the 1950s. Other *Peanuts* characters include Snoopy, Linus, Lucy, Schroeder, and Sally. More than the other characters, Charlie Brown seems to face some pretty big obstacles in life!

For one, Charlie Brown repeatedly struggles with trying to fly a kite, only to have his kite devoured by the "Kite-Eating Tree" over and over. The tree, known as "Kiteus Eatemupus," has a personality of its own. The tree is not anchored to the ground, can gobble up inanimate objects, and once showed up at Charlie Brown's door much to Charlie Brown's dismay!

The Tree even devoured Schroeder's piano on one occasion. But the Tree is best known for eating Charlie Brown's kites, sometimes lemon-flavored kites and sometimes strawberry-flavored. It seems that almost every time Charlie Brown tries to fly his kite, his kite ends up tangled in the Tree and is promptly eaten! "Poor Charlie Brown," you might say.

Once in 1958, Charlie Brown actually got a kite to fly before Kite-Eating Tree could eat it, only to have the kite combust in front of him! But kite flying is not Charlie Brown's only challenge. He never gets Christmas cards or valentines, and he only receives rocks when he goes trick or treating on Halloween. Charlie Brown is the manager and pitcher for the ball team, and their team never wins. Their all-time record was 2-930! "Poor Charlie Brown!"

Every autumn Lucy promises to hold the football so Charlie Brown can kick it. Except for once, Lucy pulls the football back before he can kick it. One time, after Charlie Brown had been sick in the hospital, Lucy did let Charlie Brown try to kick the football, but he kicked her hand instead. How discouraging! To finally get a chance to kick the ball and fail! "Poor Charlie Brown," you might say again.

Even though life does not go well for Charlie Brown, *he never gives up!* Even though he becomes sad and discouraged over and over, *he keeps on going!*

Have you ever felt like Charlie Brown, like things keep going wrong for you? In life, you too probably face many "Kite-Eating Trees," not literal trees that gobble up your kites, but other struggles that have the potential to discourage you. Flat tires, cars or lawn mowers that will not start or damaged roofs from windstorms! Refrigerators or air conditioners that quit! Irritations, challenges, and things that are not on our agenda, not in our budget, and not in our plans. Another snag, another "Kite-Eating Tree."

Perhaps your Kite-Eating Tree is facing an illness, dealing with pain or an injury. Or worst of all, you lose a spouse, a family member, or close friend by death. Being alone or losing a child was definitely not on your road-map of life—not what you would have expected. You may find your life in shambles, and the pain may be excruciating. Memories, regrets, or an intense longing to be with your loved one may make your heart ache.

Sometimes our children or grandchildren struggle in life, and we worry about their safety, their health, and their decisions! Challenges, snags, and those Kite-Eating Trees always seem to be waiting with snarled limbs ready to reach out to grab us!

After the death of a loved one there are so many things to learn, new challenges with which to cope, and less energy. You could probably make your own list of snags in life, your Kite-Eating Trees that threaten your finances, your health, and challenge your determination to keep on going! *But what other choice do we have than to keep on going?* If you give up, the Kite-Eating Tree just might win.

Sometimes problems cannot be avoided—some of the snags are beyond our control. But other times there *are* things that we can do—things such as paying attention to our health, trying to eat better, and exercising more. Friends, faith, and prayer can also give us a big boost!

We may be challenged, but, no, we are not powerless! Like Charlie Brown we must not give up—we must keep going! And a few of those Old Kite-Eating Trees might just be disappointed when there are no kites to munch!

*"There are things that we do not want to happen but have to accept, things we don't want to know but have to learn, and people we can't live without but have to let go."*
—Author unknown

# Broken Heart Syndrome

On the morning of February 28, 2006, my husband died after a long bout with cancer—a rough morning of sad good-byes. About 1:00 that afternoon someone asked, "Where's Daisy?" Daisy was our St. Bernard, my husband's dog.

I replied, "I don't know," and we proceeded to look for her. We found Daisy lying against the back of the house, and it was obvious that she was not well. Her breathing was shallow, and she was not responsive. We called our veterinarian who soon arrived. He examined her and told us she would not make it through the day.

We carried Daisy to the barn and put her on a bed of hay. My family all said our goodbyes to Daisy, and the vet gave her a shot to ease her from this life. I still wonder "Did Daisy die of a broken heart? Did she somehow sense that my husband had died that morning? Was my husband's death just too much for Daisy to bear?"

Throughout time there have been many stories about animals dying of broken hearts after a mate or someone they loved had died. Elephants mope, walk with their heads down, and their ears droop after a loss of another elephant. They have also been known to cry tears after a death.

But what about humans? Can humans die of broken hearts? According to researchers from Johns Hopkins University and Mayo Clinic, humans *can* die of broken hearts although it is a rare occurrence. Physicians can diagnose the phenomenon through EKGs, chest X-rays, and echocardiograms. Decreased functioning of the heart can actually be seen through tests even though there is no actual heart blockage with Broken Heart Syndrome.

Other stressful events besides death can set this syndrome into motion—events such as being involved in a car wreck or being robbed. Even a happy event such as a surprise party can make one vulnerable.

A person with Broken Heart Syndrome may arrive at an emergency room with shortness of breath, chest pain, and low blood pressure, mimicking the symptoms of a heart attack. The heart might be out of rhythm or pumping poorly as a result of a large amount of adrenalin or stress chemicals being dumped into the bloodstream after a stressful event.

Patients with Broken Heart Syndrome may require hospitalization for a week or so while medications are given to help the weakened heart muscle pump more forcefully. The good news is that deaths from the syndrome are rare, it is treatable, and the heart is not usually permanently damaged. People with Broken Heart Syndrome *do* recover—they *do* survive to live productive lives.

If you have ever experienced the loss of someone you love through death, you may have felt like your heart would break. You may have experienced that heart-rending, gut-wrenching emotional pain of a loss. But remember, even with Broken Heart Syndrome, hearts usually heal. With the passage of time, your pain will begin to subside as you find your new "normal".

So hang on! Go ahead and cry if you need to—tears are healing. It may not be easy to fathom right now, but you will again be able to lift your head and look the world in the face. So push through your grief. Consider some new possibilities—consider a new dream. Your heart will beat properly again.

*"Sometimes I wish I were a little kid again. Skinned knees are easier to fix than broken hearts."*

—Author unknown

# A Bumpy Ride

*O*ne early December a few years ago, I flew to San Antonio, Texas, for a week-long training—from Kansas City to Dallas-Fort Worth, then on to San Antonio. The trip was pleasant and uneventful. The training was great, and in the evenings I enjoyed the River Walk and the Christmas lights.

It was soon time to return to Kansas, and when I boarded the plane in San Antonio, it was raining. Despite the weather, our plane made it to Dallas-Fort Worth without problem.

When we arrived at Dallas-Fort Worth Airport, I had to change planes to board a plane headed for Kansas City. That plane was fully loaded—every seat was filled. I was assigned a seat in the rear of the plane—the very last row in the tail.

It was still raining, and the pilot came on the intercom and instructed the passengers to "buckle up." He said, *"Hang on! It's going to be a bumpy ride!"*

The stewardesses took their seats in the back of the plane near where I was sitting, and I heard them quietly discussing the weather forecast which did not sound good.

The plane taxied and took off into the pouring rain. Lightning flashed in the sky, and the winds blew! The pilot again came on the intercom and instructed all passengers, including stewardesses, to remain seated during the entire flight!

There would be no snacks, and no one was supposed to exit their seats for *any* reason—not even for a bathroom break. One man in the back of the plane defied the "don't unbuckle" directive as he left his seat and almost ran to the bathroom. He was pale, and I believe he was possibly nauseated!

The plane bumped and tossed in the turbulence. The wild bucking movements of the plane were particularly pronounced in the tail of the plane, and I wondered if the tail would break off!

*It really was a very bumpy ride*, but we made to Kansas City and landed safely. We were a bit worn, a bit thirsty, and in need of bathroom breaks. But *we made it*, and we were thankful!

When my husband died of kidney cancer, that was the beginning of my "bumpy ride." If you are reading this, you too may be on a "bumpy ride" due to a loss. I wish that I could wave a magic wand and take away your pain and fears, particularly your loneliness, but I cannot.

What I might suggest:

1. Grieving is not easy.
2. It's going to be a bumpy ride, so buckle up, and hang on.
3. You can do this!
4. You have to—what other choice do you have?
5. Take care of yourself—eat as well as you can, drink plenty of water, and sleep as much as you can.
6. Give yourself time to heal at your own pace, in your own way.
7. Look for little things you can enjoy along the way.

8. Allow others to help you as your "plane" bumps around.
9. It does get easier.
10. Life will be different, but life can be good again.

Grieving can be a bumpy ride. Your "plane" may land a bit tattered, but you can make it! Storms do pass, and the sun is always shining above the clouds. It's just hiding, waiting to peek through.

*"The little reed, bending to the force of the wind, soon stood upright again when the storm had passed over."*

—Aesop

# Roller Coasters

*oller coasters!* These two words bring many different memories and emotions to mind! Fun and delight for the thrill-seeker *or* apprehension, fear, and down-right terror for others! The feeling of being out-of-control once buckled into the car, knowing you cannot get out until the end of the ride! The "what's-coming-next" feeling as the cars make their way slowly *up, up, up* the steep incline with their slow *clickety-clack, clickety-clack.*

At the top of the first hill, the slow *clickety-clack* is replaced with a fast roar as the cars plummet downward, from the peak to the bottom in seconds, to travel *up, up, up,* then *down, down, down,* one descent after another.

My first real roller coaster ride was many years ago in St. Louis at the Highlands Amusement Park which housed the highest roller coaster in the U.S. at that time. I was a country girl from Tennessee who had never even *seen* a roller coaster, and my first ride is one I will *never* forget!

With the first deep straight-down plunge, I screamed with fright, and my heart raced. Then I just hung on for one hill after another, scared beyond belief. At the end of the ride, I exited that terror machine with wobbly knees, vowing I would never do that again! And I, *by choice*, have never ridden a roller coaster of that magnitude again!

When a person loses a loved one, in a sense, they board The Grief Roller Coaster. There is not usually a choice of whether or not to go for the ride. The situation forces the person on a ride of emotions associated with grief which may be very frightening. The emotional hills and valleys may be very steep, and the ride may be rough with ups and downs, twists, and unexpected turns.

Emotions may range from "I think I can, I think I can," as in "The Little Engine" story, to feelings of despair. Emotions may range from feeling on top and coping at one moment, to plunging downward due to a memory, a song, or for no apparent reason at all.

Even though there is no choice of *whether* to ride The Grief Roller Coaster, one need not feel totally out of control. Even within the situation, we as human beings *can* make some choices which may be helpful.

Shortly before my husband Ralph died, he reminded me of what lay ahead for me after his death. He knew it would not be long until he would make his journey to Heaven, and I would be grieving his death. So in an effort to help take care of me, he reminded me that grief has steep mountains and deep, deep valleys.

He reminded me that the steep mountains and deep valleys begin to flatten out a bit, turning into hills rather than mountains. The waves of grief become less frequent, are more gentle with fewer twists and turns, fewer hills and valleys.

During the steepest part of my grief ride, I found that walking and exercising helped. Having a friend I could call really helped. Staying busy helped. Looking for someone worse off helped.

I also deliberately looked for music that made me feel happy. I avoided music that made me cry. I gave myself permission to celebrate holidays, albeit very differently. I set new goals for the future. Yes, I tried to think *future*, since I could not control the past.

You may be on a Grief Roller Coaster that you did not choose. But by no means are you totally at the mercy of the ride. Consider what makes you feel less sad and alone and do more of those things. And do less of the things that make you experience the feelings of fear and despair.

You can look forward to the day when the ride will be more like riding a gentle wave than riding a machine of terror! Tell yourself, "I think I can" make it. Time *is* on your side. Even though it may be frightening, you *can* make it through your grief roller coaster ride.

"*I find the great thing in this world is not so much where we stand, as in what direction we are moving….. we must sail sometimes with the wind and sometimes against it…but we must sail and not drift nor lie at anchor.*"
—Oliver Wendell Holmes, Sr.

# Climbing Mountains

*t*he snow on the mountain range took on a warm red glow as the sunrise shone on the snow-capped peaks of the Sangre de Cristo Range near Westcliffe, Colorado. The mountains were named Sangre de Cristos, meaning "the blood of Christ," by a Spanish explorer in 1719 almost three hundred years ago when he too was awed by a similar sunrise.

Our family lived in the sprawling valley below the Sangre de Cristo Mountains in the 1970s. In early mornings and late evenings, we watched the beautiful sunrises and sunsets on the mountains. We also kept an eye out for signs of storms, flashing lightning or dark-blue streaks that stretched from fluffy dense thunderheads to the ground—signs that rain might be headed to the valley floor. So we appreciated the beauty of the Sangre de Cristos, but respected the ruggedness, the fierceness of the mountains.

We recognized some of the peaks of the range—Horn Mountain where Horn Creek Ranch nestled on the side of the slope and Crestone Needles, the sharp jagged peaks that jutted skyward, simply called "The Needles" by the locals. Then there was Hermit Mountain, wider and less beautiful than some of the other peaks, but formidable—a mountain that my husband and I tried to climb more than once.

Compared to many other mountains, Hermit Mountain is a little mountain, standing only 13,350 feet high. But to two untrained mountain climbers, it was a large looming obstacle. We would drive our old van as far up Hermit as it would go, then try to hike to the top.

As the road wound its way upward above the tree line, the oxygen was thin, making it difficult to breathe. There only short, scrubby bushes could survive. But in spite of the challenges, in the short time we lived in Colorado, we kept trying to climb that mountain, hoping to look down at the valley from the top.

When we moved back to Kansas from Colorado in 1975, we still had not climbed to the top of Hermit Mountain. Then one summer we decided to return to the Sangre de Cristo Range to camp, to once more try to conquer Ole Hermit.

The day we decided to climb was beautiful with blue skies and crisp cool air. We managed to travel higher than we ever had in our old van. When it finally groaned and stalled, refusing to go any higher, we parked and continued upward on foot, my husband climbing ahead of me.

As I walked, I could hear my heart pounding in my ears, and I could hardly breathe. "*One foot at a time, one foot at a time,*" I told myself. The top of Hermit Mountain was close, in sight. I thought "I think I'll *finally* make it this time!"

Then I heard my husband calling for me, "Hurry, come quick!" I was an EMT at the time, so I continued my ascent as fast as I could. A man was lying on the ground—chest pain, sweaty, an ashen color, and short of breath. We knew we must get the man "down below" to medical help—fast!

My husband contacted the ambulance service below—an ambulance would meet us. Then the man, his wife, and I started down the mountainside with the wife driving. A few miles down, we met the ambulance, and I accompanied the man to the clinic.

That day was the last time I tried to climb Hermit Mountain—the time I *almost* made it! As a result of my brief mountain climbing adventures, I learned how physically challenging mountain climbing can be. But in the years to come, I would have other mountains to climb, not physical mountains, but rugged mountains, nonetheless.

After my husband died, I learned how difficult mountain climbing can be, not real mountains like Hermit Mountain, but metaphorical mountains. I learned that grieving is like climbing a formidable mountain with boulders, storms, and ever-changing terrain. I learned that even though grieving is hard, the storms do move on; the weather does slowly clear. And I have learned that the view at the top is worth the climb!

*"The secret of getting ahead is getting started.*
*The secret of getting started is breaking your*
*complex overwhelming tasks into*
*small manageable tasks, and then starting*
*on the first one."*
—Mark Twain

# The Big Pit

*a* cold stinging rain hit us in our faces as we hurried toward the entrance of the Big Pit, an old coal mine in Blaenafon, Wales. Even though I was wearing three layers of clothes, I shivered from the cold. In its prime, the Pit was a bustling mine worked by about 1,300 miners until it was closed in the early 1980s to the disgruntlement of the miners. The mine is now a national historic site, a demonstration of past Welsh coal mining heritage.

I sat with my husband, daughter, and four grandchildren on a long bench, awaiting our turn for the orange steel cage that would take us to the bottom of the pit. When our turn finally came, we were instructed to remove our watches, cell phones, and cameras, anything with a battery that might spark and cause an explosion if methane gas was present in the mine.

We gave up our valuables which were locked away until our return to the surface. Next the staff passed out hard hats and wide leather belts with eleven-pound batteries—a heavy load for our youngest seven-year-old grandson. The batteries would power the lights on our hard hats while we were in the mine.

Next we were instructed to turn on our headlamps, and we were packed into the large steel cage "like sardines," as the old saying goes. Our cage slowly rattled its way downward, descending 300 feet into the earth. The air was still cold and moist, and water could be heard dripping. But we were out of the wind and stinging rain.

Our tour guide was a short, round-bellied, grey-haired

man with a ruddy complexion. Perhaps in his younger years he was "*a ginger*," a term used to describe someone with red hair in Wales. He spoke with a heavy British accent, and I had to listen carefully to understand what he was saying.

He was a coal miner until the mine closed. With a tone of bitterness, he blamed Margaret Thatcher, former prime minister of the UK, for the closing of the mine. In earlier years he said that pit ponies, children, and canaries also spent time in the mines with the men.

The pit ponies pulled heavy loads of coal through the tunnels, living most of their years in semi-darkness. About once a year the ponies were taken to the surface for a week or two where they had to wear blinders until their eyes adjusted to the sunlight.

Some children as young as four worked in the coal mines, opening and shutting the doors to the tunnels, making sure there was proper ventilation. The children also cleaned up the manure from the ponies since the methane from the manure might cause an explosion. Sometimes the children were tied to their work stations so they would not wander off if their lights went out. Caged canaries served as methane detectors. If methane crept into the mines, the birds quit singing and died. So the miners listened for the birds' songs, a reassurance that the air was safe.

The ceilings in the tunnels were low, cold, and wet. For the miners, the Pit was a place of long days and hard work, a threat of cave-ins and explosions. And if the miners' lights went out, it was a place of total darkness!

For a demonstration, our guide instructed all of us to turn our headlamps off and move our hands in front of our faces. We could see nothing—it was pitch black, total darkness, and it was a relief to turn our lights back on! Total darkness must have been horrible for the miners, but especially for a young child!

After about an hour the tour was over and our group was again packed into our orange cage. The door clanged shut, and we safely rattled our way to the surface. Our phones, watches, and cameras were returned, and we were back to familiar surroundings and the light.

In some ways, losing someone you love can be compared to going into and out of the Big Pit. In other ways, it is very different. After a death, we probably will not return to our same familiar life, and grieving may not end with a snap! Our lives may be forever changed, leaving us to question who we are and if there is still a purpose for our lives.

Real or imaginary, we may feel threatened to our very core, and depression may temporarily set in. Hopefully we will not remain in the pit too long, and our sadness will gradually dissipate as we readjust to our new reality.

As Ecclesiastes says, "To every thing there is a season, and a time to every purpose under the heaven. A time to be born; a time to die…A time to mourn, and a time to dance." While you are grieving, take good care of yourself. Be patient—grieving is hard work. Allow yourself time to heal, time for that orange cage to clatter its way back out of the Pit, to the surface, and back into the light.

*"Death is not extinguishing the light; it is putting out the lamp because dawn has come."*
—Rabindranath Tagor

# Those Autumn Leaves

*M*y father died on October 31 many years ago. His death left a big hole in my heart, and I missed him terribly. A year after his death, my oldest sister Joy and I traveled to Tennessee, the state where we were born, to visit my father's burial site and to remember him.

Joy drove from Kentucky, I drove from Kansas, and we met in our family cemetery plot in Santa Fe, Tennessee. The sun was shining, the sky was blue, and the air was warm. When we arrived at the cemetery, we were greeted with a breathtaking sight!

Throughout the cemetery there were several tall deciduous trees that were showing off their spectacular colors of red, yellow, and orange. Some leaves were still clinging to the limbs, while fallen leaves had blanketed the ground with a carpet of colors.

Other leaves were still dancing gracefully downward with a gentle breeze escorting them to their resting places. The leaves *crunch*, *crunch*, *crunched* under our feet as we traipsed around the cemetery together.

Neither Joy nor I have ever forgotten the beauty of those autumn leaves that October day! We will never forget our trip to remember our daddy. Somehow the beauty of the leaves, their vivid colors, helped take away some of the sadness in our hearts, at least briefly.

Each year as autumn replaces summer and cool air replaces the heat, the leaves show off their brilliance. But have you ever wondered how those autumn leaves turn from green to their brilliant autumn colors? Did you know that the bright colors are there all the time, just waiting to be revealed?

To give a simple explanation, as photosynthesis decreases in the fall due to cooler nights and less sunlight, so does the chlorophyll in the leaves. Chlorophyll is the chemical that gives leaves their green color during the summer. As the chlorophyll decreases, the leaves show off their reds, oranges, yellows, and golds, their true colors underneath the green!

The oak trees turn red, brown or russet. The hickories turn a golden bronze, and the aspens turn their bright yellow! Dogwoods turn a purplish red, and some maples turn bright scarlet, others red-orange. In the autumn many tourists visit the northeastern United States just to see the fall foliage!

Just think about it! The brilliant colors of the leaves were there all the time! Their beautiful colors were just covered up, buried from sight by chlorophyll. As the autumn season begins to emerge, so do the beautiful colors!

Sometimes we compare the changing seasons to the times of transitions and losses in our lives. When someone we love dies, we encounter situations beyond our control, and our hope for the futures we had planned may be gone. During those times, it may feel like winter, and it may be difficult to look forward to the springtime.

As we reach the autumn of our lives, accompanied with sicknesses and deaths, the light may seem decreased, and the future may loom grey. We may be challenged to re-evaluate our purpose in life and try to make something good come from our losses. Through our experiences we may discover what we are *really* made of and discover we are stronger than we ever imagined!

Even though there may be a marked sadness in your heart, look a little deeper. Like the leaves, you may be surprised at your own colors, your talents and capabilities that may be hidden there. You may be stronger than you ever dreamed. And maybe there are new adventures, good things waiting for you as you rebuild your life.

Like the autumn leaves that conceal their real colors with the chlorophyll, maybe a new life is waiting for you to explore, just waiting to be revealed.

*"Death leaves a heartache no one can heal,
love leaves a memory no one can steal."*
—from a headstone in Ireland

# The Lesson
# from Phoebe

*P*hoebe is a long-legged, galumping, slurping, St. Bernard. She is sweet, has big brown eyes and is as tall as a horse (almost). She has a special way of attentively looking at a person, cocking her head from side to side as if she can understand what is being said.

I became acquainted with Phoebe about three months ago after my daughter and son-in-law decided that I needed a dog, for company and protection. Initially, I was excited to get a puppy, but the puppy had to come from a family in Iowa, many miles away. Consequently, "the puppy," which I named Phoebe, continued to grow during the waiting period, and by the time I got her, she was stood at least 3 feet high, was clumsy, and literally would almost knock me down in her exuberance.

I soon found out that I really did not have time to properly care for a dog due to my long work hours and busy schedule. My son-in-law Sky and I built a very large outdoor pen for Phoebe before she arrived. I bought doggie toys for her, and very early in the morning or very late at night, I could hear the toys squeak as Phoebe tossed them around.

Even though Phoebe was fed, given fresh water, and talked to each day, by the time I got home at night there was little time to let her out of her pen to romp, which was what she really wanted. I increasingly worried about the fact that Phoebe really needed a different home, a home where someone would have more time and attention for her.

So I started the search for a new home for her. I asked people at work, I asked friends, I asked my family to help me find a new home for Phoebe. I had several inquiries about Phoebe, but I was concerned that she would be on a chain, confined to a small area, or used for breeding. In my heart I felt like I had just not found the right home for Phoebe.

With winter coming soon, I was growing increasingly concerned about the need for a home for Phoebe and prayed for God to help me find her a home. This week, I had a message on my answering machine from a lady named Sarah, inquiring about my puppy dog. When I called Sarah back, I asked why she wanted Phoebe. Sarah explained that she helped train therapy dogs and asked if she could come by that morning, and I agreed.

When I met Sarah, I knew it was right for Phoebe to go with her. Sarah explained that Phoebe might end up at a school with the children as a "therapy dog." I was thrilled at the thought of Phoebe being a therapy dog since I too have worked with children and continue to work with a program for infants and toddlers. Sarah told me that I could come to Phoebe's graduation when she was permanently placed, probably the next summer. I was thrilled with that possibility!

After Sarah left, the reality of the situation hit me. I had prayed for a good home for Phoebe, but never in my wildest dreams could I have imagined something *so* good for her. Phoebe would have a home and would be loved 24 hours a day. But even better than that, Phoebe would also have a purpose—a real purpose for her life! What more could I have asked for Phoebe?

I realized that even though the past years for me have been tough with my husband's illness and death, God still loves me, and perhaps He has a plan for me. The lesson from Phoebe is that if God is so concerned about helping me find a purpose for Phoebe, my long-legged, galumping "puppy," He must also love me.

Perhaps His plan for me will be beyond my wildest dreams, better than I can ever imagine. Maybe I just needed to relax and go along for the ride.

*Written the summer of 2007, a year after my husband Ralph died.*

*"I walked a mile with Pleasure*
*She chatted all the way,*
*But left me none the wiser*
*For all she had to say.*

*I walked a mile with Sorrow*
*And ne'er a word said she,*
*But, oh! The things I learned from her*
*When Sorrow walked with me."*
—Robert Browning Hamilton

# The Night of the Wooly Booger

$\mathcal{M}$y "Wooly Booger" experience happened in the springtime in 2007. My husband Ralph had died the previous year, so life had been a bit tough. Prior to my husband's death, it was he who I would call if there was a crisis, he who would pray with me over the phone or in person. But after his death, even though things had not been easy, there had not been a major crisis in my life until "The Night of the Wooly Booger."

Here's the story. One evening after work, rather than go home to an empty house, I drove past the road where I lived toward a town about 25 miles away. There I ate a quick meal, then went to Wal-Mart. I really did not need to buy anything in particular, but it was easier to push a basket around Wal-Mart than go home alone.

But while I was in Wal-Mart, my son-in-law Bryan called to let me know that my daughter Misty was in the hospital in another town about an hour and a half away. Her body temperature was very low and she had excruciating abdominal pain. He said the doctor was not sure what was going on. So I hurriedly exited Wal-Mart and told Bryan I was on my way.

Thinking I might need to stay the night at the hospital, I stopped by my house which was one mile off the highway to pick up a change of clothes and some cosmetics. When I drove in the driveway, I didn't bother to turn off the car engine and did not shut the door on the driver's side. I quickly gathered a few things, jumped back in the car, and started driving again.

Shortly after leaving home, I called my dear friend Joan and told her Misty was in the hospital. I told her that normally Ralph would be the one to pray for Misty, but, as she knew, he was gone. I tearfully asked Joan to pray over the phone for Misty, and she did.

It was a jet-black night. As I drove eastward toward the hospital, my mind was still spinning. But I felt reassured by the prayer of my friend. When I was a few miles further down the road, I sensed that I was not alone in the car. Then I felt something very big, very heavy, warm, and wooly move over into my lap. The wooly thing just plopped there!

I could feel the hair on my head stand straight up! A shiver went up my spine, and goose bumps popped up on my arms! It was too dark to see *what* my traveling companion was! But I did know for sure that I was terrified, and "the thing" had to go!

I started rolling down my window, putting on the brakes, then the blinker, slowing down, and moving the car to the shoulder of the road—a wonder I did not wreck! The "wooly booger" still sat firmly in my lap, heavy, furry, and warm. I actually thought I had a large raccoon in my lap—it was so big! I said aloud to "the thing," "You've got to go!"

When I almost had the car stopped, "the thing" spoke with a timid *"Mee-ow!"* You guessed it—it was a cat! When the car came to a halt, I opened my door, and "the wooly booger" bolted out of the car like a streak, quickly disappearing into the dark night!

Then I called my friend Joan again. She must have thought I had lost my senses! The first time I had called her, I had been crying, but this time I was laughing so hard I could hardly tell her my story of "the wooly booger." By then, it had occurred to me that "the wooly booger" was probably the neighbor's cat which regularly made visits to our house.

In retrospect, the whole incident made sense. The cat probably saw my car door open when I ran into the house and had crawled into the car. In the dark, I did not see the cat in the car with me, and we had traveled down the road together for several miles. Perhaps I scared the cat as much it had scared me!

A few days later, I spotted the neighbor's cat in our yard again. The cat had found his way back home! But that experience with the neighbor's cat taught me some lessons:

- I learned the importance of having a wonderful friend to pray with you when there is a crisis. (My daughter was having a gall bladder attack, later had surgery, and was fine.)
- I learned that some of those "things that go bump in the dark" are not always monsters as we might think. (They might be something as harmless as the neighbor's cat.)
- I learned that "laughter is the best medicine" in a crisis. (Laughter can make you forget your tension—forget your tears!)
- *But most of all, I think God must have a sense of humor. When I had my encounter with "the wooly booger," I can imagine God looking down at my situation. I believe He cared for me during my crisis, and I can imagine God having a good chuckle too!*

*"The human race has only one really effective weapon and that is laughter."*
—Mark Twain

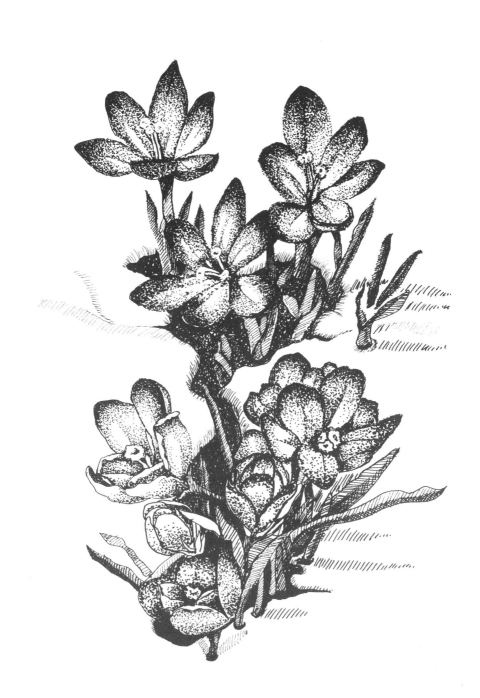

# Springtime
# and Geese

*H*onk, *honk, honk, honk*, the lonely sound of geese over-head, winging their way south in autumn. *Whirr, whirr, whirr*, the sound of flapping wings and honks move across the sky, become faint, and are gone. The cold north wind urges them onward, and they fly on and on, day and night.

Winter is right behind them, and instinct tells them they must fly south. Perhaps their *honk, honk, honk* could be translated *hard, hard, hard*, and their flight is hard indeed! At night their mournful *honks* and *whirr* of wings are clues that geese are flying in a cold dark sky.

When you hear the sound of geese in the daytime, you may look up and see a flock of geese flying in a *V* forma-tion, sometimes symmetrical and sometimes not-so-perfect as they struggle against buffeting winds. *Hard, hard, hard*, they may be crying. But on and on they fly with those in the back honking encouragement to those in the front.

Maybe they are saying *go, go, go* or perhaps they are saying *on, on, on*. At times a goose from the back of the *V* will move to the head of the *V*, giving the tired leader a break. Due to the *V* formation, all the geese can travel 71% easier than alone. The bird immediately in front of another goose provides uplift for the goose behind him. Their unique fly-ing pattern makes flying easier for each goose.

If a goose is wounded during the journey, two other geese may drop out of the *V* and accompany the wounded goose to the ground. They will stay with the sick bird until the goose dies or is well enough to travel again. If the wounded goose survives, the three of them may then join a new *V* of travelers and continue the journey.

Most geese mate for life and live for about twenty to twenty-five years. Each spring geese migrate two to three thousand miles to return to their home in the northern U.S. or Canada where they were hatched and reared.

In the spring when the geese journey north, the air may still be crisp and cold. But each fall and spring, nature calls, and they retrace their paths of many miles, in the fall to escape the cold of winter, and in the spring to anticipate hope of new life, a new family.

When the south breezes begin to blow in the spring and the buttercups and forsythia display bright-yellow colors, I imagine the honks are saying something totally different than in the fall. Their honks bring anticipation of new life and *hope, hope, hope.* Hope of returning to their home territory. Hope of new baby goslings, for a cycle of life to begin again.

The spring after my husband died the flowers still blossomed, and the geese honked their way north. In previous years I had looked forward to spring with excitement welling up inside as I eagerly watched for signs of spring. But after he died, that first spring, there was no joy, no hope for better times. It was difficult to even think of life without him. And if it had not been for friends and family, I might not have made it.

In difficult times we may need our friends and relatives to help make our way a bit easier. Like the geese, traveling *with* someone is much easier than traveling alone. Friends, in a sense, can lead the way, push against the wind, and give uplift on our journey.

In nature, the cold, hard winter eventually gives way

to buttercups and spring-green leaves. And the winter of grief usually turns into spring, a time of hope for something better, a season without dark skies and harsh winds, for springtime and *hope, hope, hope.*

*"Hope is the only bee that makes honey without flowers."*
—Robert Ingersoll

# A Person's Gotta Do What a Person's Gotta Do

When our grandson Will Thomas was about four years old, Will and I were chatting over our backyard fence with our neighbor Lori. I cannot recall what prompted the statement that Will confidently said to Lori. But it was a big thought for such a little guy, and he used it appropriately. To my surprise, Will announced to Lori, "A person's gotta do what a person's gotta do!"

After that backyard-fence talk, my husband Tom and I have chuckled more than once when we have thought about Will's words. And we have made the statement to each other in various situations—"A person's gotta do what a person's gotta do."

And I think that old saying can also apply to someone who is grieving. After a death, there are many "gotta dos" to get done. Decisions to make. Paperwork, bills to pay, thank yous to send. Visits to Social Security, businesses to notify of the death, addresses to change with the post office. And bigger decisions to make such as what kind of gravestone, how to get finances in order.

But how a person grieves following a loss may be as individual as each person's beliefs, personality, background, and coping style. Whether it was an unexpected death or one following a long illness may affect how we grieve. Some may have already grieved their loss, at least partially, before the actual death of their loved one if the illness was pro-longed and the death unusually painful. No matter what, grieving hurts!

The age of the person who died can also impact how those left behind grieve. For instance, if a child dies, the death of a child is not the natural order of things. And the loss of a child leaves a gaping hole in a young family, rob-bing parents of their dreams for their child.

The relationship of the one grieving with the deceased can make a big difference too. For instance, if the deceased was abusive to the surviving loved one, the one left to grieve may feel mixed emotions—relief that their abuser died, but guilt for feeling relieved, as well as sadness if they cared about their abuser.

No two persons grieve exactly the same or at the same pace. Some people need to talk about their loss more than others. Some benefit from bereavement groups, and some do not. Some are angry, and some are not. Written information may be helpful to some, but not to others.

Some feel the need to visit the grave often, and some do not. Some can get rid of clothes or change the room of the one who died soon after the death, and some can-not. Some are ready to move on and take on life sooner than others. Some choose to stay close to home; some choose to avoid being at home. Some like to listen to music and some don't. The same music or different music may be helpful.

Consider what would make life easier for you. And let your family know what you need. How you grieve is up to you, and you can make some choices. So treat yourself well, even pamper yourself a bit. And don't feel guilty for taking care of yourself.

How you grieve is up to you. You are in charge! No

rights, no wrongs. A **"person's gotta do what a person's gotta do,"** backyard-fence advice from a four-year-old.

*"Have regular hours for work and play;*
*make each day both useful and pleasant,*
*and prove that you understand the worth of time*
*by employing it well."*
—Louisa May Alcott

# Black Tulips

*I*n the springtime buttercups, violets and tulips brighten our world with their many-colored blossoms, but tulips probably show off the largest variety of colors. There are Red Dynasty tulips, Apricot Beauties, Burgundy Lace, Pink Diamond, and Emperor Whites. Yellows, oranges, purples, multi-colored and even blacks. Black tulips—a very different color for a flower!

More tulips are grown in the Netherlands than any other country in the world. Massive fields of tulips grow in profusion in the spring—a sight to see! But tulips did not originate in the Netherlands; they were brought to the Netherlands from Turkey in 1593. After their arrival in the Netherlands, the country experienced what became known as "tulip mania." Tulips became so valuable that the bulbs were sometimes stolen from gardens or used in place of money!

Tulips were brought to America in the 1800s by Richard Sullivan, a rich man who owned 500 acres in Salem, Massachusetts. It is interesting that tulips from Europe were first grown in the U.S. in Salem, Massachusetts.

During the Salem witch trials of the 1600s, Salem was a place of suspicion, hysteria, fear, and deaths. Several were sentenced and hanged. Many were accused and imprisoned—sad times! So Mr. Sullivan's bright-colored meadows of tulips of the 1800s were a remarkable contrast to the dark history of Salem in the 1600s!

You may be wondering what black tulips have to do with loss and grief. Black tulips are associated with beauty, power, and strength. They are also a symbol of farewells and are used in floral arrangements for funerals, usually with other bright-colored flowers.

Black tulips are noticeable and unique, interesting flowers indeed. They are also strikingly beautiful—alone with their silvery green leaves or in other flower arrangements. The lighter-colored flowers make the tulips look even blacker, and the black tulips make the other flowers look even brighter—sharp contrasts!

*Mysterious*, *intriguing*, or *interesting* might be some words to describe black tulips. Yet in reality, they are not truly black. They just appear black, especially in dim light, due to their very deep purple, deep red wine or dark maroon colors. Maybe you have wondered, "Are black tulips natural or are they hybrids?" And the answer is, "They are hybrids," developed after much trial and error in the early 1900s. The Queen of the Night is the most cultivated black tulip. It grows taller than most tulips, some up to 34-36 inches tall. It also blooms later than many of the bright-colored tulips.

Perhaps grief is similar to the black tulips—dark on its own, but not yet truly black—there are glimmers of other colors. For even in times of grief, if we look around, we will probably find some bright flowers—friends and family who care. Those who give hugs, send cards, and offer caring words. So, like the tulips, maybe grief is not all totally black after all, even though it may feel that way.

Perhaps we would never see the contrasts of bright things around us if it were not for the blackness of grief. Perhaps we would not appreciate good health and marvel at each new day if we had not lost someone we loved.

In order for any flower to grow there must be sunshine, rain, and the darkness of the soil around its roots. Growth begins as the roots draw strength and nutrients from the dirt. Tulips must be planted by fall to experience the cold of winter before they can emerge tall, proud, and bloom beautifully in the spring. After a loss, we too, like the black tulips, can bloom again—it just may take some time.

So look around for the flowers. People, like flowers, can provide some brightness in your life, so let them help. Like the black tulip, a symbol of strength, you are probably stronger than you ever thought you could be. So search for ways to grow through your grief experiences. Even black tulips show off different colors in the sunlight—beautiful purples, deep rich reds, and maroons. Remember black tulips are not truly black after all.

*"People are just as happy as they make*
*their minds up to be."*
—Abraham Lincoln

# A Desert
# in Bloom

Covered wagons lumbered along, heading west, as weary travelers looked forward to "better days" and the gold in California. The year was 1849—the Gold Rush. Many families from the Northeast had loaded their possessions and families into the slow-moving covered wagons, risking their money and lives. Their journey was not easy as they crossed prairie, mountains, and deserts in search of a new life, and many graves marked the wagon trails, ominous warnings to those following.

Some of the "Forty-Niners" traveled in the San Joaquin Company wagon train which left Salt Lake City in October, 1849, after stocking their wagons with supplies for the journey. It was getting late in the year to cross the looming Sierra Nevada Mountains, and the tragic story of the Donner Party who had tried to cross the Sierras about two years before was still fresh in travelers' minds. The Donner Party had been caught in a snowstorm and believed to have resorted to cannibalism in a futile attempt to survive.

The San Joaquin Company wagon train could only travel as fast as the slowest wagon, so some in the party decided to strike out on their own on a southerly route, following a fictitious map with a short-cut which was supposed to save them time and miles.

But they encountered unexpected obstacles on the way—gaping canyons to cross, not enough water to drink, and more. So by the time they arrived in the desert of Death

Valley, it was Christmas Eve, 1849, and food was scarce. Some slaughtered their oxen, used their wagons for firewood, and cooked the meat into jerky. From there on, they would have to traverse the desert on foot.

Some pioneers in the wagon train decided to send two young men across the mountains for supplies, and wait for their return. Others decided to keep moving in spite of the heat, and lack of food and water. But even with the hardships, only one older man in the San Joaquin wagon train died in the desert.

When the Forty-Niners crossed the desert, they probably faced a brown, dry terrain with treacherous, shifting sand. So it was probably hard for the weary travelers to imagine anything beautiful *ever* emerging from the desert, of all places. After successfully reaching the other side of the desert, while looking back from a mountain, one man supposedly proclaimed, "Good-bye, Death Valley!" thus giving Death Valley its name.

But when the setting sun and evening shadows mingle in Death Valley during the winter, the sand dunes take on a breathtaking orange glow as the desert is transformed into a spectacular scene of beauty! And in the spring, with sufficient rain, some *real* surprises emerge in Death Valley. Bright colors begin to pop up across the desert with flowers pushing their way through cracks, between rocks, and through the sand.

Flower seeds which may have lain dormant on the desert floor for months or years begin to sprout and grow! Blossoms of blue lupines, yellow California poppies, and daisies add their brilliance, and violet sand verbenas show off their colors. Blue bells, wild snapdragons, evening primrose, and desert marigolds! Ocotillo cacti add their splash of orange-red blossoms as the desert literally comes alive with flowers, birds and desert critters—about 400 species of birds live in Death Valley.

In life we also experience difficult times when someone we love dies, our own Death Valley experience. We too may look for short-cuts through grief, longing to bid the sadness of loss good-bye. And after a death it may be difficult to believe that life will ever be good again, hard to expect that beauty and happiness will ever replace the aches in our hearts.

But we must hope that our life, our desert, will someday grow and bloom again. Hope is like the dormant seeds in the desert sand, just waiting for the right time, the right environment to grow. Even though we may feel an urgency to move through our strange, frightening desert to a better life, we must remember that grief rarely kills us, even though it can make life excruciatingly painful and difficult.

Grief, like the desert, can bring blinding, shifting sands and apprehension. But if we had never experienced a loss, maybe we would not appreciate the beauty that life brings after the storm has passed—a springtime bursting with color—a desert in bloom!

Clouds and storms are needed to bring the rain, and rain is necessary for seeds to sprout, for flowers to grow. So cling to your seeds of hope. Be patient. Believe that your desert will bloom again, and don't forget to *watch for the flowers!*

*"The pain passes, but the beauty remains."*
—Pierre Auguste Renoir

# Dandelions

*I*n June of 2009 four of my sisters and our husbands drove to Alaska, traveling the ALCAN Highway through Canada, a 1,700-mile stretch of road from the U.S. to Alaska. We drove long days on mountainous, winding roads, over roads with rough patches caused by the freezing and thawing of sub-zero winter temperatures.

We drove above timberline. We drove in the rain. It was a long hard trip, but it also had its rewards. We saw mountain goats and mountain sheep up close! We saw baby bears with their mothers. What a thrill!

Once when we stopped to take pictures of a mother bear with her twin cubs from the car, the mother bear threateningly ran toward our vehicle. She was fast! I was afraid and cried out to my husband to "Go, go!" as I frantically rolled up my window. The car moved forward just as the mother bear reached the edge of the blacktop.

But one of the most remarkable things about the high country of Canada was the dandelions. If there had been no dandelions, there would have been no flowers at all growing in that cool, thin air.

At first, we were not sure what we were seeing! The tall, bright yellow flowers resembled dandelions, but they were *so* tall and *so* big—growing in such unlikely places! But they *were* dandelions—the tallest, most beautiful dandelions we had ever seen! They were growing in patches, above the tree line, surrounded by dry, rocky land with little other vegetation—where the winters reach forty below zero.

Right there at the top of the world were splotches of bright yellow color as patches of dandelions stood proud and strong. The dandelions were a bright sight in contrast to the dry, barren mountainside! They were surviving where no other flowers were growing!

After that trip through Canada, I have not looked at dandelions the same. I used to think of them as pesky weeds that mar the beauty of a freshly mowed lawn as their fluffy white heads pop up, replacing the yellow blooms. I only saw them as a nuisance, not a beautiful flower. But now I have new admiration for the lowly dandelion. They are resilient; they *can* add beauty!

They are tenacious. They can grow and survive in a harsh terrain in climates where other flowers cannot. Their bright flowers are pleasing to the eyes of both children and adults. Dandelions can become a bouquet when picked by a child for a parent. Or they can provide intrigue and entertainment for small children who blow away their fuzzy white heads after they have bloomed.

If someone you love has died, you might feel very alone in your new harsh, rocky terrain. Perhaps you have felt there is nothing you can do to contribute to the world. You may have been shaken to the core after your loss. But give yourself some time to heal.

No matter how old we are or what we have gone through, all of us have something to offer. We have learned many life lessons. Experiencing loss probably makes us stronger and wiser than before. Like those dandelions in Canada, there are ways that we can contribute and brighten the world around us.

You have gifts to offer. So be tenacious. Be deliberate as you sink your roots deep into life again in search of moisture and warmth to nourish you. Live each day well. Each day is a gift. Like the dandelion, turn your face to the sun, stand tall and proud, and grow!

*"If we had no winter, the spring would not be so pleasant."*
—Ann Bradstreet

# Dancing in the Rain

A few years ago, soon after my husband's death, I received a beautiful plaque which I promptly placed in the kitchen as a daily reminder of the importance of squeezing as much out of each day as possible. The words on the plaque read:

> *"Life isn't waiting for the storm to pass,*
> *It's learning to dance in the rain"*
> —Vivien Greene

But how does one dance in the rain when life is physically or emotionally painful? How does one keep moving when he or she is facing a life-limiting illness or even death? And how does a person face the future without someone he or she loved so dearly?

George Gershwin wrote the song "Summertime," a song about easy living. Some of the words are: "Summertime, and the livin' is easy, fish are jumpin', and the cotton is high." With words and musical notes, Gershwin painted a picture of life that is relaxed, peaceful, with a soon-to-be-harvested crop. No stress, good weather, and plenty of money to be made. Life is good!

But life as described in this famous song is sometimes very different from what we actually experience. There are storms, natural disasters, accidents, financial strains, illnesses, and aging that stress us, challenge us. And when someone we love is diagnosed with a life-limiting illness, our comfortable life may immediately turn into a nightmare, an emotional storm.

One day our life may be going well, and the next we may be facing storm clouds and rain. That was the case with Gershwin, the composer. By the age of fifteen, he was recognized for his musical talents and was in demand. Some described him as a musical genius.

He had an opportunity to study music, and composition came easily for him. Some of his famous works were "Rhapsody in Blue," "Porgy and Bess," "Embraceable You," and "They Can't Take That Away from Me."

When he was at the peak of his career, he moved to Hollywood and was hired to compose the music for the movie "Shall We Dance," starring Fred Astaire and Ginger Rogers, both famous for their dancing abilities. It was then at the age of 37 that Gershwin's life fell apart. His future was ripped away, and he was unable to complete the music for "Shall We Dance."

Gershwin began experiencing headaches and strange symptoms. When he was diagnosed with a brain tumor, he underwent surgery. Doctors tried to remove the tumor, but Gershwin died during the surgery at the age of 38 years. He lost the opportunity of living into old age. Songs that he might have composed if he had lived a long life were never written.

Sometimes illnesses or accidents rob us of our dreams, and lives are shortened. Some of us will never have the opportunity to write a book, compose a song, or spend time with grandchildren as they grow up.

When my husband was diagnosed with kidney cancer, we realized that we would not be able to retire together—that dream was gone. And one of my husband's biggest fears was that the grandchildren would not remember him—they were very small when he died.

When someone we love dies, those of us who are left behind are challenged to fill the holes in our aching hearts and find new meaning in life. In a sense, we are left in the midst of an unpredictable storm.

But how does one dance when he or she can scarcely eat, sleep, or stay on their feet? You may still need some time before you are ready to dance. But if not now, maybe later, life will be easier and you will feel like dancing.

So for right now, do what you can to keep living. Be patient and give yourself some time. Try to believe that someday you will dance again. And whatever you do, don't put away your dancing shoes.

*"To every thing there is a season,*
*and a time to every purpose*
*under the heaven:*
*A time to be born,*
*And a time to die....*
*A time to weep, and a time to laugh;*
*A time to mourn, and a time to dance."*
—Ecclesiastes 3:1-4

# A Surprise in the Middle

*M*y sister Hope handed me an almost-round object with a look of excitement in her eyes. It was about three inches across, rough to the touch with gouges and chips on its dark-grey surface. The gouges were a lighter grey color, and it was held together with a wide rubber band.

The spherical object was heavier than I had expected. I had an idea *what* it might be since my sister and her husband had been to Iowa for a dig. Wearing their rubber boots, they had slogged up and down hills in the mud as they searched for buried treasures.

Hope said, "Open it," and on closer examination I found that my "rock" had been cracked into two pieces which fit together almost seamlessly. I took off the rubber band, pulled the rock apart, and held the two pieces in my hands. The inside of the object was very different from the rough, ugly rock-like exterior.

The partially hollow middle was lined with jagged, sparkly crystals. Some of the crystals were tiny, others were large. Some were white, some light grey, and some darker grey. They were irregular, with larger clumps and smaller clumps—all beautiful, shimmering and sparkling in the sunlight! I was looking at the inside of a geode, ugly on the outside and beautiful on the inside—a treasure from my sister Hope.

Geodes form over thousands of years and usually require volcanic activity, hot water, and a variety of minerals which help determine the final colors inside the geodes. But first there must be a hollow bubble which hardens into an empty cavity. Then, over time, hot water seeps into the cavity carrying minerals which form the beautiful crystals inside.

Pressure, heat, the right soil, and cataclysmic activity are needed for the formation of geodes—the beginning of something beautiful. Even though most crystals are quartz, some of the crystals are multi-colored barite, pyrite, dolomite, amethyst, and jasper, a treasure hunter's delight!

Perhaps geodes are like people with rough-looking and tough-acting exteriors. Many have experienced some difficult situations in life, and their outward beauty may not be apparent. The pressures of life may have helped mold them, filling their hollow cavities with either bitterness or good. Illnesses, relationship problems, and deaths may gouge us and roughen us up, molding us into someone different than we would like to be.

The hurt from losing someone we love can cut deep into our hearts, causing us to build imaginary walls to protect ourselves from future hurts. And when we are hurting, it may be difficult to realize that we have the opportunity to grow as a result of our pressures and hurts. It is hard to realize that our empty cavities, our empty lives, may someday be filled with something beautiful.

So after a loss, hang on during those the high-pressure times. Take care of yourself physically, spiritually, and emotionally. Maybe there is something good, something beautiful in the making!

*"Ordinary riches can be stolen;*
*real riches cannot.*
*In your soul are infinitely precious things*
*that cannot be taken from you."*
—Oscar Wilde

# He Died
# Laughing

*Q*uestion: *Do people actually die laughing?* According to history, some may.

In 2003 a 52-year-old ice cream salesman died laughing, according to his wife. She reported that her husband had started laughing in his sleep, and she could not awaken him. He laughed so long that his doctor believes his heart stopped or that he died of asphyxiation.

History also records the story of a man from Denmark who began laughing while watching a funny movie. His name was Bentzen, and he laughed until his heart rate increased so much that he may have died of cardiac arrest.

In 1975, another man named Alex died after watching a "Kung Fu Kapers" episode. He laughed so long that he died of heart failure. It is believed that he may have had a pre-existing heart condition.

A few others have died while laughing, but the incidences are very rare. And even if a person should "die laughing," I ask, *"What a way to go?"* Could death be any more pleasant than that? For those who have seen a loved one die an agonizing death, to "die laughing" might have been a good exchange.

Research has found that laughter is good for humans. The Bible says a merry heart does "good like a medicine." And some studies have verified that laughter can help fight off illnesses and help boost the immune system, prompting Laughing Clubs that have sprung up around the United

States. People just get together and laugh—that's the agenda for the meetings—to laugh.

Norman Cousins, a writer and editor of the "Saturday Review," is a good example of someone who put the laughing theory to a test after he became ill with an extremely painful collagen disease. He began a regular program of laughter, watching funny videos. He found that if he could belly-laugh 10 minutes, he could get at least two hours of sleep. And he literally laughed his way out of a painful, crippling disease.

One study tracked heart attack patients for a year after their attacks. They were divided into two groups. Both groups received medical care, but one group was asked to watch comedy for 30 minutes a day. At the end of the year, the laughing group had lower blood pressure than the group with only medical care.

To sum it up, here are some benefits of laughter:

• Laughter increases our endorphins, our "happy" hormones.
• Laughter is contagious—it is hard to not laugh when someone else is laughing.
• Laughing is an activity you can enjoy with someone else.
• Laughter reduces pain.
• Laughter decreases blood pressure, increases circulation, and carries more oxygen to the cells.
• Laughter decreases stress.
• Laughing for a few minutes can help you feel better for hours!
• Laughter gives the immune system a boost.

After the death of a loved one, those left behind may actually feel guilty for laughing, fearful of forgetting their loved one. But this is not true. You will never, ever forget the one you loved! So do not be afraid to laugh, to look for the funny things in life—funny songs, funny movies, jokes, and light-hearted stories. Laughter is good medicine for a grieving heart!

Search out people who are fun to be around, those who build you up, those who make you laugh. More than likely you will never be one who "died laughing." But even if you were one of those extremely rare ones, I say, "What a way to go!" Enjoy life. Life passes far too quickly, so laugh.

*"With the fearful strain that is on me night and day, if I did not laugh, I should die."*
—Abraham Lincoln

# Bumblebees and Hollyhocks

*I* grew up in Tennessee on a farm where my sisters and I were free to safely explore our large back yard, woods, and beyond. We romped barefoot from early spring until fall, making memories to last a lifetime. One of my memories is of bumblebees and red hollyhocks.

Let me tell you how it worked. When the hollyhocks were in full bloom in our back yard, my sisters and I would pick off a big blossom, just the flower without a stem. We would hold the blossom in one hand like a cup and face the hollyhock stalk with wide-open blooms, waiting for an unsuspecting bumblebee to arrive inside a flower to sample the sweet nectar.

When the bumblebee had settled himself inside the flower, we would quickly clamp the already-picked hollyhock over the blossom on the stalk with the bumblebee inside. Then we had to *hold on tightly, really hold on,* to the two flowers to keep the bee trapped.

While we held on to the hollyhocks, the bumblebee inside became frustrated and buzzed and buzzed, louder and louder! We had trapped a bumblebee, and we were in charge of the show! Such fun it was—at first!

Then, in time, our arms became tired, the game grew old, but the very angry bumblebee was still inside the hollyhock. Yes, the only down side to our game was that *we eventually had to let go; we had to turn the bee loose!*

Even though we had done the "bumblebee-hollyhock

trick" enough times to know the bumblebee usually won, it was always a temptation to do it again. We had learned to run like crazy when we let go, but we usually got stung! The pain was excruciating with ensuing swelling, soreness, and itching to follow!

Looking back, I believe there are lessons I learned about bumblebees and hollyhocks which can be contrasted and compared to grieving.

- As children we chose whether or not to play the bumblebee-and-hollyhocks game. With grieving, there is no choice.
- Sometimes when playing with bumblebees and hollyhocks, we did *not* get stung. Grieving almost always causes excruciating pain.
- As children, while hanging on to the hollyhocks, our arms became tired; hanging on to the past can also become wearisome and tiring.
- Whether hanging on to an angry bumblebee in two flowers or hanging on to the past, turning loose of either can be painful. (Turning loose and moving on with life does not mean you love the one who died any less.)
- When holding on to a bumblebee, one must make a decision *when* to turn loose. The same is true with grieving the loss of a loved one—we can make some conscious decisions about when to move on.

Letting go of your grief can be difficult, painful, and even frightening. You may be afraid that if you try to move on and leave some of the pain behind that you will forget the one you loved—you won't forget.

When I was a child, letting go of that hollyhock was really scary. I knew that, more than likely, I would get stung—that it would be a painful experience. But there was no way that I could move around the yard and play as long as I had my hands clamped over the two hollyhocks.

Even though letting go of grief can be difficult and painful, at some point, one may have to turn loose of the "hollyhocks" and let the bumblebee go in order to move forward in life and build a new future. And only you will know when the time is right for you.

So dare to kick off your shoes and feel the cool, green grass beneath your feet. Maybe there are some exciting experiences waiting out there just for you. Yes, *sometime you just have to let go!*

"*When one door closes, another opens;*
*but we often look so long and so regretfully*
*upon the closed door that we do not see the*
*one which has opened for us.*"
—Alexander Graham Bell

# Just Playin'

"Come here, Tom! I can't believe what I just saw!" I excitedly said to my husband Tom one morning last summer. I had been watching two little rabbits from our kitchen window. Tom soon joined me, and I told him, "One of those little rabbits just hopped straight up in the air, and the other one ran *under* him!"

As Tom and I watched, sure enough, Rabbit Number One stopped a few feet from Rabbit Number Two as if waiting. Then Number One ran toward Rabbit Number Two as if to startle him. Then Number Two jumped straight up in the air while Number One ran *under* him while he was airborne!

We could hardly believe it! They repeated their trick several times. I could almost hear Rabbit Number One saying, "All right—get ready, get set, *now jump!*" They finally seemed to tire of their game and took off down the alley together. I wish I had a video of their rabbit game to prove what we saw. It might have "gone viral" as the saying goes— it was such a fun scene!

If you have watched young puppies or kittens, you probably know that most baby animals like to play—like to chase, frolic, roll, and tumble. I have also watched squirrels chase one another up a tree or birds playfully swoop and dive at each other in the air. But I had never seen rabbits do such a trick, repeating it several times!

After that morning, I thought about those two little bunnies playing and about how children also like to play.

Little girls play and seem to be practicing for when they will someday be mothers. They swaddle their babies in blankets and pretend to feed them.

Children "play house," usually designating a younger child to play the role of "baby." They pretend to do the things they have seen adults do—sweeping the floor, washing clothes, or running the vacuum. Playing is fun for a child, but it is also how they learn. Play is their work! So children play for fun *and* to learn.

But why do baby animals play? Scientists have studied little animals, trying to answer that question, but maybe there is no deep, dark answer. Some scientists have concluded that animals play "just because it is fun"—a good-enough reason!

As we grow older, we sometimes lose interest in playing as we settle into the routines of work and life. It is easy to let responsibilities fill our free time, and we forget to have fun as little children and baby animals do. And after the loss of a loved one, playing may be the farthest thing from our minds.

Sorrow can almost take over our thoughts and lives. We may find our minds dwelling in the past, reliving our memories of the one who died. The past may, in a sense, swallow up our present and block the possibilities for pleasure. We may feel guilty for laughing or believe that we should not have fun after a loved one dies.

But having fun is good for us, even after a loss, good for us physically, mentally and emotionally. Play can reduce stress, help restore the body, and may even help reduce the risk of dementia. So it is just as important to take time to play as it is to work!

Even if we avoid "playing," we cannot bring back the one we loved. So why not schedule some time to play, to do something you enjoy? Doing something fun might be a way to make new friends and strengthen your body physically, mentally, and emotionally.

So why not play "just because it is fun?" We may never jump high or run fast like the little rabbits, but it is important to play in whatever way we choose. So think about what you enjoy doing and move ahead with life. And don't feel guilty for "*just playin'*."

*"It is a happy talent to know how to play."*
　　　　　　　　　　　—Ralph Waldo Emerson

# The Ice Cream Cone

*i* watched as a thin, wrinkled older man slowly licked his ice cream cone, turning the cone from side to side, cautiously eying it for any melting drips of ice cream that might silently escape. I remembered eating an ice cream cone like that when I was a child in Tennessee, when ice cream cones were a nickel, when nickels were scare, when ice cream was a rare treat to savor.

I was watching that older man while sitting in a booth at a restaurant in a town not far from home. That night I was avoiding going home to an empty house after my husband had died. My booth was fairly close to the older gentleman who was soon joined by a second older man, taller, heavier, and better dressed.

The second man addressed the ice-cream-cone man. "Well, how are you doing?" he asked. I remembered the face of Man #2—I had seen him at Wal-Mart one night about mid-night, pushing an empty cart around the store the same as I had been.

"I'm doing fine," the man with the ice cream conc replied, as he carefully licked his vanilla treat as if trying to make it last as long as possible.

"But are you getting enough to eat?" the second man pointedly asked.

"Yes, I went to the senior meal at noon today."

Second man, "But I worry about you. Are you sure you are doing okay?"

Those are the snip-its from their conversation that I remember. Even though it has been over eight years, I have never forgotten that scene. Now, as then, I still admire Man #2 for his caring, gentle spirit and how he genuinely seemed concerned about his friend.

And I have since wondered, "What had life been like for Man #2? Why was he pushing an empty cart around Wal-Mart at midnight? Could he not sleep or was he avoiding an empty house like I?" I wondered about the older man's story, but I did not have the nerve to ask.

I knew my story—I dreaded being home alone because my husband was no longer there. And I had learned that if I stayed up late until I was very tired, then I could go home, fall into bed, and sleep a few hours, without thinking.

I still have nagging questions about Man #1 with the ice cream cone. "Did he really have enough to eat? Was he sick? Why was he so thin?" He had seemed proud, reluctant to accept help, declaring he was "fine."

If you have ever watched people in a mall while waiting for someone, maybe you have studied the faces of those hurrying in and out of the stores. Perhaps you have wondered, "Who are they? Where are they from? What are their stories?"

Each of us has a story to tell. Some of our stories begin with fairy-tale weddings and end with distrust and betrayal while others are of love, wealth, and success. Some end with the untimely deaths of those we love, and our hopes and dreams are dashed. *But everybody has a story!*

Perhaps your life story has not turned out as you had hoped it would. Maybe, against your wishes, the ending to your story was revised when someone you loved died. But since you are alive, you have an opportunity to add a new chapter to your life, to write a new ending.

So as you "write" your story, remember to be kind—to care about those around you as Man #2 did. Even if we light a small candle for someone else, we are shining a little light on our own path.

Consider a quote by Gautama Siddarta, written hundreds of years ago. "Teach this triple truth to all: A generous heart, kind speech, and a life of service and compassion are the things which renew humanity." Be kind to others along the way—it will help *your* heart heal. And make your own story a good one!

*"Do all the good you can
By all the means you can,
In all the ways you can,
In all the time you can
To all the people you can,
As long as ever you can."*

—John Wesley

# The Scissortail

*i*t was the Wednesday before Memorial Day, 2006. My husband Ralph had died on February 28 of that year. It had been my goal to have his gravestone in place before Memorial Day, and the monument company met the goal.

On that day, my children, grandchildren, and I gathered at the cemetery to remember Ralph and to see the new arch-shaped gravestone which I thought was appropriate for Ralph since he was from St. Louis.

It was a warm, sunny day—a perfect Kansas day with a gentle breeze. The wheat was *swish, swish, swishing* in the field across from the cemetery while our family checked out the new gravestone.

My grandson Will Thomas was just a baby, about one year old at the time. When Will saw Ralph's photo on the back of the gravestone, Will reached toward the picture, touched it, and said "Papa." Even though he was very young, he had not yet forgotten his grandpa who he called Papa.

While we were still in the cemetery, a bird with a very long split tail flew past me and my grandson Sam, age 9, and lit on another gravestone. After a brief pause, the bird then flew a short distance and lit in a small tree. Prior to that moment, I had never seen a scissortail, but I *knew* that was what the bird had to be—a real live scissortail!

Seeing that bird was very significant to me, and I will share why. My late husband's favorite movie was "The Trip to Bountiful," released in 1985, starring Geraldine Page who received an Academy Award for her performance.

The movie is the story of an older woman named Carrie Watts who lived in a small apartment in Houston, Texas, in the 1940s with her son Ludie and his wife Jessie Mae who liked to drink "Coca Colas" and visit the beauty shop. Jessie Mae only tolerated Mother Watts living when them because she liked to spend Mother Watts' pension check.

In the movie, Carrie wanted to return to Bountiful, Texas, where she had lived in her earlier years *just one more time* before she died. On various occasions Carrie Watts had tried to run away to Bountiful, but the daughter-in-law usually foiled her plan.

But on one particular day, Carrie out-foxed her daughter-in-law and took a bus to her deserted, ram-shackled house in the country near what used to be Bountiful. While there, Carrie went inside the house and visited room by room, reflecting, remembering her life there with her husband and young son Ludie.

While walking the pasture near the home place, Carrie reminisced about the birds that have lived near her home in years past. She debated with herself about her favorite bird—the red bird, the mocking bird, or the scissortail? And Carrie finally settled the issue with a statement, "*I don't know anything prettier than a scissortail flyin' through the sky!*"

On that day in the cemetery when I saw a scissortail for the first time ever, I felt the same way—that scissortail was a beautiful sight to see! But it was more than just seeing a scissortail for the first time. It was more like a connection, an affirmation, a reassurance.

My grandson Sam and I felt like Ralph *knew* his family was there remembering him. There could not have been "*anything prettier, than a scissortail flyin' through the sky*" on that Wednesday. Perhaps it was Ralph's sign to us—his reassurance that all was well—that he was up there *"flyin'"* too! It was a special time and a milestone on my road to healing.

After the death of your loved one, you have probably honored your loved one by placing a just-right gravestone. And hopefully you have told stories about your loved one to keep memories alive. If the stories brought tears, tears are healing. Or maybe your story-telling brought laughter, but laughter is good medicine for the soul.

If you have experienced a special incident or reassuring dream about your loved one, you are not alone. Many have experienced such occurrences after a loss. As for me, I will never forget that special day when there was nothing *"prettier, than a scissortail flyin' through the sky."*

*"In the night of death, hope sees a star, and listening love can hear the rustle of a wing."*
—Robert Ingersoll

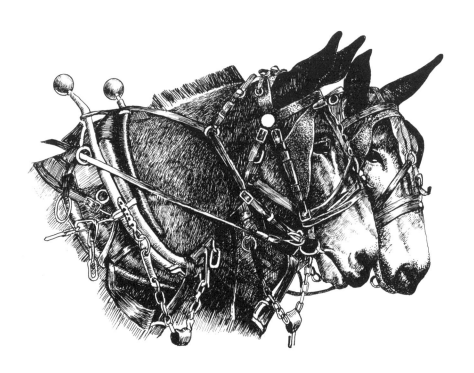

# Laying
# It By

"Pappy," my grandfather, trudged along behind a plow pulled by two mules in the beating-down sun in Tennessee, readying the soil for the tobacco plants that he would soon plant. He wore faded overalls as he and his mules worked the field.

He owned six mules total. There was Mandy, Bell, and Bill; the names of his other three are long forgotten. Pappy preferred his mules to the new shiny tractors that were being driven by some of the other farmers, doggedly clinging to his old ways.

A large tobacco barn lay to the left side of the long driveway leading to my grandparents' large two-story with its wrap-around porch. By fall I knew the barn would hold the up-side-down stalks of tobacco that had been cut, strung onto tobacco sticks, and hung in the barn to dry. After curing to a yellow-brown color, the tobacco would be hand-stripped from each stalk, leaf-by-leaf, and sent to market. But I am getting ahead of the story.

I grew up in a time in Tennessee when growing tobacco was a good cash crop, before research proved the correlation between tobacco and cancer and before the danger of the pesticides used on tobacco was known. During my childhood, even children helped dust the white poison onto the tobacco plants to kill the huge creepy tobacco worms that chomped away at the tobacco leaves.

The 4-inch-long worms were actually larvae which

would soon become hornworm moths. The green worms were squishy with white stripes and black horns protruding from their posteriors—an ominous sight for anyone who is squeamish. Children and adults worked in the tobacco fields, hand-picking the worms off!

But that too is ahead of the main point of this story. To begin with, tiny tobacco seeds were planted into a long seed bed, usually in February. The bed was covered with strips of long, white fabric, usually cheesecloth, to protect the young plants from the cold. After the threat of frost, Pappy planted the young plants called *"tobacco slips"* in the field that he had tilled with his mules.

As the plants grew, the rows were hoed to rid the tobacco plants from weeds, and a cultivator on wheels pulled by mules turned under the weeds in the middles of the rows. The process helped destroy some of the tobacco worms that would otherwise devour the tobacco leaves— the worms ate the leaves mostly from the underside to avoid the light of day.

Later the plants would bloom, showing off beautiful pink or white flowers. But the blossoms were not allowed to stay long—they had to be "topped" to remove the flowers and re-route the nutrients into the tobacco leaves. New green shoots called "suckers" appeared, replacing the removed blossoms, but they too had to be plucked off, leaving a sticky residue on the hands of those who removed the suckers.

At just the right time, Pappy did his final plowing of the field before the plants were too high, before the leaves spread out in the middles of the rows. That final plowing had to be done while it was still beneficial, not detrimental, to the plants. When he did the last plowing for that summer, he called it *"laying it by."*

His plowing was *done, finished, complete*, even though other steps were needed before the crop made its final trip to market. When Pappy and the other farmers *"laid it by,"* that phase of their work was out of their hands. Any further plowing would only harm the crop, and from then on, the plants must survive the weeds on their own.

Even though I have not heard the term *"laying it by"* used by farmers since moving to Kansas many years ago, I believe that Kansas farmers, like Tennessee farmers, must, at some point, be finished with plowing their crops, when the corn or milo is too tall to cultivate. The farmers' final plowing is *done, finished, complete*, and it is time to *"lay it by"* and try not to fret, but trust Mother Nature to do her part.

There are other times in life that we must *"lay it by"* and let things go—a time to say, "I have done all that I can do with this situation or relationship and to do more might bring harm." Some situations or people cannot be changed, and we must leave things in the hands of Someone higher than we.

Especially after the death of someone we loved, it is easy to second guess how we have lived our lives—to have regrets about working too much, for not taking enough time, or regrets about things we did or did not do. But some things can never be changed, and the only direction left to go is forward, toward the future, not backward to the past.

We have battled the "weeds," fought the obstacles, and plowed our "field" for the final time. Sometimes there is nothing else we can do but forgive ourselves and move forward, even though self-forgiveness can be difficult. But beating oneself up for things that cannot be changed can be harmful to one's self and to others.

So if you have regrets, think of my Pappy cultivating his field that final time, of turning his crop over to Nature and to God. Lay your regrets aside. Forgive yourself and determine to live well in the future. *"Lay it by"* and move on.

*"Never look back unless you are planning to go that way."*
—Henry David Thoreau

# A Different
# Kind of Christmas

*I*t was late afternoon when my airplane landed in Fairbanks, Alaska. My sister Joan met me at baggage claim, and we headed out of the terminal. A cold blast of air hit my face, and I immediately felt the hairs in my nose freeze—a strange sensation! Even though my sister had warned me it would be cold, and I was wearing layers, a scarf, and gloves, I was not prepared for the frigid weather.

The blast of 30-below air cut through me as I was introduced to a land of frozen tundra, snow, ice carvings and twilight in December—a totally different world than Kansas. My sister had invited me to spend Christmas with her family in Alaska that year in an effort to help me get through my first Christmas and anniversary after my husband's death. She knew it would be difficult for me to repeat our traditional Christmas meal at the farmhouse without my husband Ralph.

So I had gone to Alaska where Joan packed my days with new sights and fun. On Christmas day there was food galore at my niece's cabin in the country. We snow-shoed, my first time, and I found that walking in snow shoes was not as easy as it looked! I saw mushers and dogsleds, ice carvings and a real ice castle, and a mother moose and her baby—my camera lens kept freezing over, making my later-developed moose photos blurry.

We drove to Chena Hot Springs about 60 miles from Fairbanks—an actual end-of-the-road location. We swam in an indoor pool then went outside to the hot springs. The water was extremely hot, and the outside 35-below air was ideal for turning the trees around the hot spring into a frosty, white winter wonderland. Our hair immediately froze white in the humid air and sub-zero temperatures, and we looked like we were wearing white caps that matched the landscape!

One afternoon my sister drove us to her cabin about 30 miles from Fairbanks. Again 35 below! No indoor plumbing. No electricity and only a wood stove. I shivered while we waited for the fire in the wood stove to heat the cabin enough so the kerosene lanterns would light. We slept in sleeping bags, still fully clothed in our coats. I was so padded I could hardly move!

But one day stands out vividly in my memory—December 28th—the day that would have been my 45th wedding anniversary if my husband had lived. As my sister Joan and I were driving back toward Fairbanks from the cabin, I could see a gold mine in the distance, and it was twilight. I was in a cold, foreign land as the sun dipped below the horizon in the almost-dark light of day. A strange sight in a cold, harsh land that is not for the faint-hearted!

My heart ached for my husband, and I wished he had been there to experience Alaska with me. But that was not possible. His death had drastically changed my life forever. Emotionally I was also in a strange, frozen land, but life must go on, just as it has for millions who have lost someone to death.

That Christmas, that anniversary—both immensely different from any I would have ever imagined. But as the sun set I realized I had made it ten months without my husband. It had been tough; there had been tears. But I had made it through a different kind of anniversary and *a differ-*

*ent kind of Christmas.* As the last bit of light left the horizon, I was pleased, I was thankful. Life *would* go on.

"*When we are no longer able to change a situation…we are challenged to change ourselves.*"
—Victor Frankl

# Some Things
# Still Remain

We called him "Pappy." He was grey-haired, tan-skinned, and wrinkled from working in the fields. He had a large tummy, just right for grandchildren to pounce on. He wore old, faded well-worn overalls that were sometimes "hitched up" with baling wire after a suspender broke. He is remembered for "fixing" grandchildren's bee and wasp stings with tobacco juice.

It was not unusual on a hot day for Pappy to come in from the hot fields in Tennessee and lay on the floor in the kitchen, using the back of a chair that he had turned up-side-down as a diagonal rest for his back while he rested on the cool, hard floor.

Pappy was my granddaddy, a man adored by all his grandchildren. His death was my first up-close experience with death as a child. When he died, I thought my heart would break. I realized that death was permanent—that I would never see him again on this earth.

My cousins and I cried until our eyes were red. The funeral home brought the casket with Pappy in it back to the "home place" for the equivalent of today's respect calls, and people "sat up" with him until he was taken to the church for the funeral and burial.

Pappy seldom dressed up, and he would not win any prizes for how he looked when he worked around the farm. But to a child, looks meant nothing. What mattered was who Pappy was. The grandchildren liked being around him and found sheer delight in jumping on his soft round tummy. We knew he loved us, and we loved him!

Looking back, I was blessed to have Pappy as my granddaddy. He died at the age of seventy-four of a heart attack while fixing fences. Even though he physically left us that day, he left some valuable gifts behind for our family, three gifts in particular.

First, he left behind **the gift of relationships**— healthy relationships with his children and grandchildren. He taught us how to trust and how to love. Even though Pappy is no longer with us on earth, our relationship with him will never end.

Pappy also left us **the gift of memories**, memories of good times with him, and what wonderful memories they are! Fun memories, loving memories! Memories of him sitting in the front yard in a big pile of yellow, red and orange leaves—grandchildren in the leaves around Pappy and a baby on his lap.

The third gift he left us is **the gift of lessons-learned**. He taught us what a relationship with a grandfather should be like. He taught us how to love, to laugh, to romp. He taught us the lesson of hard work, honesty and integrity. He taught us that outward appearance is not as important as what is inside a person. When he died, we had to learn to grieve, to experience the pain of loss as children, with cousins leaning on cousins. But he also taught us to remember the happy times, to cherish our fun memories.

If you have lost a loved one through death perhaps they too left you these gifts—the gifts of relationship, of memories, and lessons-learned. Yes, even though our loved ones leave us and move to the Other Side, *some things still remain!*

*"When someone you love becomes a memory,*
*the memory becomes a treasure."*

—Author unknown

# Don't Be Afraid to Move On

Let's take an imaginary trip to the savannahs of southeast Africa to learn about impalas, a graceful animal categorized by National Geographic as antelopes and taxonomists as gazelles. They are reddish-brown in color. The males have horns, and the females do not, but both have distinct black and white stripes running down their rumps and tails.

Impalas are agile and fast, very fast! And they can jump 8-10 feet high and easily leap 30 feet in a single bound! They can reach speeds of 50 miles per hour and can run zigzag patterns at a speed of 37 miles per hour. Their phenomenal speed and ability to jump come in handy when they are pursued by predators such as cheetahs, leopards, and lions.

But there is one thing that seems to set impalas apart when they are put behind a wall in captivity. A wall 3 feet high in a zoo can keep them inside—they will not jump over walls! Ironic, isn't it? They can jump 10 feet high in a large field where they can see everything around them. They have the capability of eluding predators at 50 miles per hour, but a three-foot wall can keep them captive!

But why don't they just jump over the wall? Physically, they are still capable of jumping. Are they captive because of their inborn instinct? I do not have the answer, but it is interesting to think about nonetheless. Maybe they are "stuck" behind the wall because they cannot *see* where they might land—afraid of the unknown.

Maybe impalas are similar to humans who have gone through difficult situations in life—financial problems, struggles with relationships, health problems, or losing someone we loved. When faced with adversities, maybe we become "stuck" emotionally, maybe a bit depressed, making it difficult to move on with life or make decisions.

Our unknowns are not visible three-foot high walls. But when we face obstacles and hurts, it is easy to become fearful of moving on with life, especially when we find ourselves in unfamiliar territory, bewildered. After the death of someone we loved, it is easy to become fearful of losing someone else, fearful that we too might die, or frightened of other ominous events that life may hold! Grief may feel like walls of fear.

After the death of his wife Joy, the famous writer C.S. Lewis found that grief can be frightening. Before his marriage to Joy, C.S. had lived a life of routines, sameness, day after day. He taught at Oxford, England, spoke magnificently, and penned many stories and books which won him acclaim.

He fell in love with Joy Davidson and married her. But their life together was short-lived. They were only married a few years before she died of bone cancer. But in their short time together, C.S. learned what it was like to love and be loved. He learned that loving someone deeply comes with a price tag. If we love someone deeply, we will grieve deeply.

Their story is told in an old movie "Shadow Land," a movie that tore at my heart. C.S. was a learned man, one of the elite of England, yet he was not spared from grief. None of us are exempt, and there are no magic "cures." If we love someone deeply, we are vulnerable. Grief hurts!

At some point in life, all of us will lose someone we loved. But since we are alive, I believe we each still have a purpose to fulfill. So consider what you would like to accomplish with your life, and take steps to move forward. Even though it may be scary to step beyond your imaginary "wall" when you cannot *see* exactly *where* you may be headed, don't let your grief hold you captive.

You can make a choice to continue life as it is now or move toward some new goals—you will know what is right for you. But if opportunities arise, even if you cannot *see* exactly *where* you are headed, *don't be afraid to move on!*

*"A man is not old until his regrets take the place of his dreams."*
—Yiddish Proverb

# Beyond
# the Hedge

*i* held my breath as my daughter Misty and I zipped down a narrow, two-lane highway near Cardiff, Wales. She was driving, and I was the passenger. In Wales the cars travel on the left side of the road which was scary and unfamiliar to me. After living in Wales for a year, Misty was accustomed to the treacherous roads, so she was calm. I was used to the straight wide roads of Kansas, so the curvy, hilly roads of Wales were frightening beyond belief!

The highway was extremely narrow, sandwiched between wide, high rock fences which formed thin corridors. The fences were sometimes higher than our car, built hundreds of years ago for horses and buggies, not for fast-moving trucks and cars! When the rock fence would end, it was usually replaced by thick hedges, making it impossible to see over the next hill or around the next curve. Sometimes trees overhung the highway like a canopy, shutting out the sunlight—a beautiful but almost eerie sight.

I squeezed my hand-grip and braced myself, fearing our car might crash into an immovable wall or an oncoming vehicle. Sometimes our car was so close to the left side of the road that the hedge actually slapped my side of the car, making me flinch or duck!

But in spite of the scariness of the trip, there were little breaks in the highway as a road jutted to the side, giving a quick glimpse at scenes which were too beautiful to properly describe. Hillsides shone golden in the bright sunlight, and lush green meadows were sprinkled with grazing sheep which were oblivious to the dangers that lay on our side of the hedge. The sheep were calm and peaceful, and life was good.

I began eagerly watching for those breaks in the hedge—those peaceful scenes. It was comforting to see the beauty concealed beyond the hedge, beyond the wall. When I focused on those little glimpses, I paid less attention to the oncoming traffic and the narrow roads, and I was less afraid.

I believe my frightful ride might be compared to life with its hills and valleys, the uncertainty of not knowing what is behind the next curve. Perhaps the rock fences with their thick hedges are like death—that final unknown—the barrier between life and what comes next.

Many of us have been taught what the Hereafter may be like, but few of us have experienced it. But there is an exception—those who died, were resuscitated, and brought back to life. There are interesting similarities in the stories told by these people, regardless of their age, background, or country.

Many tell of leaving their bodies, of watching the scene below as doctors or nurses scurry around, working on their bodies. They report trying to let those in the room below know they are there. Many patients tell of traveling down a tunnel, then seeing a bright light, a light which does not blind or frighten them, and of seeing loved ones who had died. They tell of feeling peaceful and not wanting to return to their bodies, but are told that their work on earth is not finished, that they must go back.

It is hard to imagine what our loved ones may be experiencing on the "other side," but it must be good! Since we are still alive, our work on this side is not yet finished. So

we must keep traveling, searching for those bright spots—
those little glimpses of heaven while on our journeys.

Perhaps death is like that rock fence covered by the
hedge—that barrier separating us from the beauty that is to
come—that world of peace and light where our loved ones
are waiting for us—waiting for us somewhere *just beyond
the hedge*.

*"While we are mourning the loss of our friend,*
*others are rejoicing to meet him behind the veil."*
—John Taylor

# Doing Good
# Is Good for You

*a* few months ago, I visited a friend in Missouri who gave me permission to make copies of some of her artwork. I asked her where I might find a copy machine, and she directed me to a business a few miles away. After arriving, I explained to the man in charge that I would like to make some copies, and he promptly brought a key to unlock the copy machine.

Then to my surprise he asked, "And what do you want copied?" as he reached for the artwork in my hand.

I asked, "Would it be all right for me to make the copies myself?" I wanted to adjust the light and dark on the machine to make sure I had clear copies.

But to my surprise, he said, "No." Then he asked, "How many?"

I replied, "One copy," and he put the first copy on the glass and pushed the button without adjusting the dark or light setting. He handed me the first copy—grayed and useless for my purpose.

One by one he reached for the next picture, making no effort to adjust the settings on the machine. It was soon apparent that I was wasting my time and money, so I thanked the man, paid him, and left. But I was steaming inside!

During that experience, it was not *what* he said, because he said little. But it was *how he made me feel*. Did he think I was incapable of using a copy machine? Or did he think I would break the machine? And why did he seem so unconcerned about the quality of the copies? I will never know, but I will never forget *how he made me feel*.

Perhaps you have been around people who have made you feel angry, hurt, or sad. Or maybe others have brightened your day, leaving you with memories you will always treasure. Recently I asked some of my friends if they have had some surprising *good* things happen to them, and here are some of their responses.

One friend, a mom, told a story of taking her sons to the circus when they were very young. She said she barely had money for the gas, tickets, and for snacks. When they got inside the circus, there were glow wands for sale.

Like any young child, her boys wanted them, but she explained she did not have enough money for toys. She said a lady must have heard what she said and bought each of her boys a glow wand, much to their delight! My friend had tears in her eyes as she recalled the memory.

A nurse friend said that one Christmas she was filling her gas tank when a man approached her and said, "I don't want to scare you, but I want to pay for your gas." She did not know the man, but she will always remember his kindness—*how he made her feel*.

Sometimes just a simple remark can make a person's day. Recently someone in a restaurant told my husband that he has "never changed" in looks. Believe me, he was beaming! It was right after his 74th birthday! He won't forget that remark!

Research has shown that we remember our negative experiences much more vividly and longer than our positive ones. The negatives are recorded in the right side of our brain, and the left side of our brain remembers our positives. It is also believed that we need at least five positives to help counteract one negative.

Research also has shown that people who do good things for other people are the happiest people of all. Even toddlers are happier when they give something away instead of getting something—well, mostly.

If you have encountered difficulties in life, some bumps in the road, hopefully you will soon be able to participate more fully in life. As your energy level increases, consider doing good things for others. And try to avoid being around those who make life more stressful for you— you have a choice.

When we help others, it reduces our own stress level and gives us a new sense of purpose and fulfillment. It helps us feel connected, more peaceful, and less depressed.

*Just remember*, we need at least five positives for each negative. And what we do for others does not need to be costly. A smile, a phone call, or offering a cup of coffee to a friend can work just fine. *Just remember, doing good is good for you!*

*"When I do good, I feel good.*
*When I do bad, I feel bad.*
*That's my religion."*
—Abraham Lincoln

# Eagles—
# Learning to Fly

*E*agles—graceful, proud, magnificent! Eagles—symbols of pride and strength. Eagles—flying at thirty miles an hour, soaring high in the air, or diving at sixty miles per hour to snatch a fish from a stream, quickly rising again!

But have you ever wondered where eagles nest or how they learn how to fly? If you are interested, let's begin on a very high cliff with a stream meandering through the valley floor. The air is crisp and cool. The sky is blue, and the day is clear with an occasional whimsical cloud floating high overhead.

On the edge of the cliff there is a large nest which was built by a male and female eagle. It is about four feet wide and three feet deep, made from limbs and lined with pine needles, soft mosses, feathers, grass, or leaves. The nest is a just-right place to rear a couple of baby eaglets!

The parent eagles usually mate for life and return to the nest year after year. They repair the nest by adding limbs and additional lining until the nest is extremely heavy—sometimes heavy enough to topple a tree if that is where the nest is built! Then the female lays one to three speckled, off-white colored eggs. In about thirty-five days, soft fuzzy eaglets will peck their way out of the eggshells.

The babies emerge vulnerable, totally dependent on their parents for food. They grow rapidly, and their once-comfortable nest becomes crowded. In need of space, the young eaglets are forced to move to the edge of the nest where they discover a new world below. "Wow! What a view!" Entirely different sights and colors—green grass, trees, water, and flowers!

The mother knows her eaglets must soon leave the security of the nest. There are new lessons to learn if they arc to grow into strong, independent eagles, and she knows they must learn to fly. The mother flies close to the nest, trying to entice the babies to join her in the air. "How scary," a little one might think or "No way am I going to do that!" as he clings to the edge of the nest!

Then the mother gradually removes mosses and leaves that line the nest, exposing the rough limbs that poke into the young birds—"Ouch!" The mother quits bringing food regularly, and the eaglets become hungry and lose weight. Then she flies by the hungry eaglets with a tasty morsel of meat. She dangles it just out of reach as the babies perch on the edge of the nest.

Motivated by hunger, the eaglets try to grab the meat from their mother's beak. And as they reach, they may temporarily become airborne for a few seconds. Next the mother may fly near the nest and gently push an eaglet out of the nest. Startled, the baby will instinctively spread his wings and flap. To his surprise, his wings may hold him up and he flies!

If a young eaglet begins to fall, the mother swoops beneath and catches him on her back. She may give him a ride, dump him, and catch him again! Flying lessons, exciting and exhilarating to the onlooker, are probably anxiety-producing and scary for the eaglets!

In life, we humans face many kinds of crises, scary times such as divorce, sicknesses, relationship struggles, financial problems, or deaths of someone we love. During these times, we are forced to make changes in our lives. Like the eaglets, our nests become uncomfortable as our soft lining, our old familiar life, is removed.

When someone we love dies, we grieve. Grieving is hard work, and we are vulnerable. We, like the eaglets, are challenged to cope, to personally grow, to develop new flying wings in our unfamiliar world.

From time to time, we may need to rely on our faith, friends, and family to catch us when we fall, to let them swoop under us and pick us up. Eventually, we, like the eaglets, will find that life can be good again. We will find a new normal. We, like the eagles, will learn to spread our wings, catch an air current, and fly.

*"With the past, I have nothing to do; nor with the future. I live now."*
—Ralph Waldo Emerson

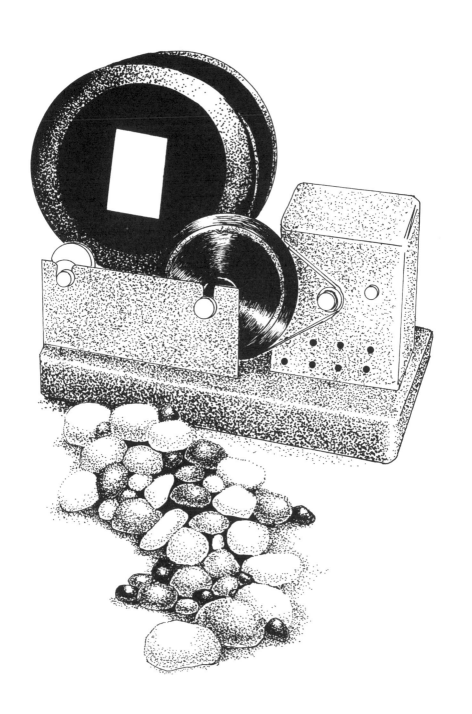

# Those Rocks Are Tumbling

For years I said, "*Someday*, I'm going to buy a rock tumbler." For years I picked up pretty rocks while on trips, bringing them home for *that* day when I would buy *that* rock tumbler. For years I bought a few beautiful, already-polished rocks while on trips—rocks which were once ugly, dull, ordinary rocks.

My husband Tom had heard my *"Someday I'm going to buy a rock tumbler"* statement—I really was not hinting. I had put off buying a tumbler for several reasons. I did not know for sure *where* to buy one; I did not know *what* to buy; I was not sure I would know *how* to operate one; I was not sure I had the *time* to tumble rocks; and the old excuse, "I don't have the *money*."

Several days before Christmas, Tom proudly placed a heavy, tall Christmas gift under our tree. He did not give me any hints other than "You have always wanted one." He said that further hints would give it away. I really had no idea what surprise awaited me in the box!

When I opened the big package on Christmas morning and pulled out a heavy blue canister, I *still* did not know what I had. I had never seen a rock tumbler, just thought it would be very exciting to have one.

But I *did* know what a tumbler could do for rough rocks—turn them into rocks smooth to the touch and beautiful to behold! I knew a rock tumbler could bring out the brilliant colors and patterns which had been trapped inside ordinary-looking rocks.

Tom and I read the rock tumbler instructions together. We chose rocks that we hoped could be transformed into something beautiful. Then we carefully filled the canister about 2/3 full and added coarse grit and water. Tom put the lid on and "snugged" it tight. Then he plugged the tumbler into an outlet, and the rocks began their magical journey toward transformation.

It was on January 9, 2011, that our rock tumbler started turning and tumbling in our basement. *Tumble, rattle, tumble, clatter*, round and round. It took over 700 hours of tumbling to smooth the rocks—four weeks—one week with coarse grit and water, one week with fine grit and water, a pre-polish grit, then the final polish!

I think we as humans could be compared to those rough, dull, unpolished rocks. We have rough edges and faults. We are imperfect and lack luster. But perhaps the purpose of life is to smooth out our rough edges, get rid of some of our imperfections, to bring out our inner beauty, so that we can help others while on this earth.

Perhaps we are like the rocks, and the tumbler is like life. Life tumbles us around a bit, up and down, around and around. In life there are some things that we can control, things about which we can make choices and decisions. Sometimes there are circumstances beyond our control—things that are out of our hands entirely, such as death.

Sometimes we have to rely on our human "grit" as well as the "grit" of people and God, to help smooth out our rough edges. Perhaps it is during the difficult times, even times of grief, when we are tumbled around in life. Maybe that is when we get our sharp edges ground off, when we learn lessons, and get "polished" so we can help others when they face similar circumstances!

While we are alive, I believe we all still have purposes to fulfill. And when our time on earth is finished, God will stop our "tumbling" and call us Home. But for now, life goes on—*tumble, rattle, tumble, clatter, polish, polish, polish.*

*"All my life I have tried to pluck a thistle*
*and plant a flower wherever the flower*
*could grow in thought and mind."*
—Abraham Lincoln

# The Goody
# in the Middle

*d*o you like Oreos? I sure do. And my daughter Misty likes Oreo—*really* well. In fact, when she was a young girl, it was a challenge to keep the Oreos hidden from her—it became a game.

There was a research study done by Connecticut College to try to determine if Oreos are addictive, and I will not go into the details of the findings. But they used rats, rice cakes, and Oreos in the study to try to prove their point.

The rats were placed in a maze where they had a choice of going for the rice cakes or Oreos. And maybe you can guess which the rats preferred. Oreos, of course, particularly the creamy filling in the middle. No real surprise!

Which would you choose—an Oreo or a rice cake? Have you ever eaten a rice cake? Dry, almost tasteless, but low in calories. A rice cake has just 35 calories—mostly carbs with 1 gram of protein. No fat, low sodium—actually not a bad snack if you are trying to cut calories, to lose weight. But enjoyable? Not very, not to me anyway.

And then there are Oreos. Two dark-chocolate cookies that sandwich the creamy white filling—that goody in the middle. A little less than 54 calories per Oreo—about 2 grams of fat, one gram of protein, and about 8 carbs. But, oh, such an enjoyable snack, especially with milk—*yum, yum!*

But isn't life kind of like eating rice cakes or Oreos? Some mundane times, some enjoyable times, and even times of extreme sadness? Sometimes we get rice cakes—

dry, almost tasteless. And sometimes we get Oreos—those enjoyable, delectable moments we long for with the goody in the middle. Like time with the ones we love, music, laughter, a good book, or sitting outside in a gentle breeze in the summertime.

After a death, we experience hurt, sadness, life with little fun, no sweetening. And the winter months don't help—cold weather, being cooped up, wondering if spring will ever arrive. And responsibilities still demand our time— bills to pay, meals to prepare, clothes to wash—chores that are not much fun.

Even while we are hurting, we have the opportunities to make choices about how to spend our time. Figuratively, we can choose to only eat rice cakes, do only the things that are not enjoyable, and life will probably be very boring and lackluster. But I believe it is good to do some things that we *enjoy* as well as the things we *must* do—a mixture of work and play. (Remember the old proverb, *"All work and no play makes Jack a dull boy?"*)

Enjoying life is good for our physical health and emotional well-being. And if you are getting older, as I am, it becomes more important to decide how to spend your time, kind of like rationing life since there are fewer remaining years.

So what will you choose to do with your time? Only boring things? Or can you slip some small pleasures into each day? Popcorn, a good book, a cup of hot chocolate, a walk on a warm day, a movie, a hot shower to relax you? Ask yourself, "What do I enjoy?"

Along with the things we *must* do, there are things that it *would be good* for us to do, such as eating nutritiously and exercising. So how are you going to spend your pre- cious time? Doing something that matters or just frittering your time away? Doing some things you enjoy along with the mundane? Make your days count, and don't forget to go for *that goody in the middle*!

*"Life…gives you the chance to love, to work, to play, and look up at the stars."*
—Henry Van Dyke

# We Grieve, We Heal, and Life Goes On

The mother barn swallow frantically flew around her nest, drawing attention to her plight. She dove, swooped, fluttered, and cried out to get my husband's attention as if to say, "Please do something! Please help!"

The nest was the home for the mother bird and her three young barn swallows when I lived in the country, when my husband Ralph was alive. The nest was not a new one, but an old nest that a mother bird had built on the side of our house in previous years. Birds had returned to raise new families in the nest year after year.

But this year something was very different. The nest was not the usual peaceful scene with baby birds peeking down at us while we peeked up at them. Something was wrong! The mother bird was setting off an alarm, crying out for help.

When Ralph carefully looked up at the nest, he could see three little birds dangling from the side with shreds of twine around their feet. The baby birds were lifeless—it was too late for him to help.

The strands of twine had ensnared her little ones and caused their deaths. When my husband saw what had happened, he came in the house and got me. We went back outside together, and he said, "That mother knows something has happened to her babies. She is grieving!"

It was obvious to us both that the mother barn swallow was in agony, and our hearts were touched by the sight. My husband promptly tore down the nest, so no other baby birds could become ensnared in the twine in the future. And after that day, my husband and I were more aware that humans are not the only ones who grieve.

Not only do birds grieve, but scientists have also observed other animals grieving by expressing a wide range of emotions after a death. For instance, when an African elephant comes in contact with another elephant that has died, the elephant may nudge the dead elephant as if to awaken him or try to lift the lifeless elephant to his feet. Some elephants have been seen stuffing grass into the mouth of the dead animal as if to feed him.

Some elephants may remain near the body of a dead friend and grieve for a full week before returning to their previous routines. Some stand silently over the bodies of their dead companions or later stroke the bones of an old friend as if they are remembering past experiences. If the parent of a young elephant has died, there are reports of the young elephant waking up screaming.

Jane Goodall who spent most of her life observing chimpanzees in Tanzania wrote the story of a young chimpanzee named Flint after the death of his mother Flo. After Flo died, Flint climbed into a tall tree and stared down into the empty nest he had shared with his mother. Flint became lethargic, refused to eat, and became sick. Eventually he slowly made his way to the place where his mother had died, curled up on the spot, and he too died. Did Flint die of a broken heart?

Many other animals have grieving rituals as well—sea lions, gorillas, wolves, llamas, and dolphins, to name a few. Wolves may display long mournful cries after a death.

Sea lions wail pitifully when whales kill and eat their babies. Gorillas may bang on their chests and howl when a companion dies. Llamas wail and dolphins mourn the deaths of their infants.

So humans are not the only ones that grieve after a loss. But animals and birds seem to return to their regular routines in a shorter time than humans, in a few days or a couple of weeks, whereas humans tend to grieve longer.

Death is a part of that cycle of life. And at some point in our lives, we will experience loss and grieve. Grief is the price of loving, the price of commitment to another person or animal. Facing death may cause us to look introspectively at our own lives and realize our time on Earth will not go on forever. Death may motivate us to search for meaningful ways to contribute to life in our remaining time.

So when someone we love dies, even as with our feathered friends and animals, wild or tame, we grieve. And hopefully we will heal from our loss, not die as Flint did after the death of his mother Flo. Most people do survive loss. Hopefully we will find hope for the future and build a fulfilling life without the one we loved. And yes, like the elephants, we will always remember. But *we grieve, we heal, and life goes on.*

*"Today well lived makes every yesterday a dream of happiness and every tomorrow a vision of hope. Look well, therefore to this day. Such is the salutation to the dawn."*
—Sanskrit Proverb

*Ralph Timothy Thorn*
*February 18, 1943-February 28, 2006*

# "Remember Me"

It was June 23, 2000, a day I will never forget. My husband Ralph was in the hospital with abdominal pain which the doctor at first thought was due to diverticulitis. But the C-T scan revealed something far more ominous.

Our doctor came into his hospital room and spoke frankly with me and my husband. He stated, "You have a little diverticulitis, but that is the least of your worries. I am 99% sure that you have a big cancer setting there."

If you have received such news, you can probably relate to the feelings my husband and I had at that moment. We felt like we had been kicked in the stomach, like the air had been knocked out of us.

The doctor said to me, "Come on, Dawn." Since I had worked at the hospital for several years as a nurse, I knew the physicians well. And I think he wanted me to know what we were facing.

So I followed our doctor down the hall to the Radiology Department where he put on the C-T scan film which showed an enormous mass in my husband's abdomen. There was no denying that my husband was facing quite a battle ahead. The mass was already outside the kidney and the organs in the abdomen were pushed from their usual positions by the mere size of the tumor.

After going back to my husband's room, Ralph and I talked. One of the things that I remember him saying is, "I am afraid the grandchildren will not remember me." He was afraid he would be forgotten.

On July 13, the cancer was surgically removed, but

within a year, the cancer had started slowly growing back. Even though there were no more medical options, we were blessed with the gift of more time. He lived to see two more grandchildren born, and two of the grandchildren were old enough to remember him after he died.

In February, 2006, shortly before he died, he again verbalized to me his desire to be remembered. He said to me, "Dolly, *remember me* when you see the sun set."

I replied, "How could I ever forget you? I will never forget you."

He also told me, "You've got to write the story." He wanted the story of his life passed down to the grandchildren. Even though his time with his grandchildren was shortened, I promised him I would write his story, and that is still my plan—parts of it are done.

Throughout the forty-four years we were married, both he and I made slides of the Kansas sunsets. He even put the slides to music for a slide show. Our common love of the Kansas sunsets was an emotional connection, and even now, several years later, even though I have remarried, when I see a Kansas sunset, I think of him—it is inescapable.

But there are many other things that remind me of my husband. I remember the first night we went out together and how he made me laugh. Coming from a strict pastor's home, laughter was important, and his sense of humor added spice and fun to our marriage.

I remember when we dated and galloped horses across cornfields in the dark. I remember swimming across the Lake of the Ozarks with him—a good half a mile across. I remember the lean years, the years we hardly had money enough to pay the bills. I remember the births of our children when he was there. I remember the many holidays with family and the cookouts in the pasture when he was the chef!

When the air is crisp in the fall, I remember how he longed for the first frost. I remember him thrilling to the honk of geese flying south for the winter; it meant that cold weather was on its way! I remember his love of living in the country and love for the mountains of Colorado.

And when I hear John Denver's "Hey, it's good to be back home again," I remember him, and still get a tear in my eye. He sang each grandchild to sleep with that song. And I remember him—the pastor, the teacher, the loving husband, the parent, and doting grandfather.

I remember the last months of his illness, "the final days" as we call them, and I am sorry life was so hard for him. He was one of the most independent people I have ever known, yet he became bedfast and had to be dependent on us for his every need. We remembered him through the funeral service and through choosing a gravestone which we believed he would like.

And even though my life has changed drastically since I remarried, I will never forget Ralph. He was the father of our children—a part of my past, my history, our history, of our children, and grandchildren. I am who I am today because of his love and influence of 44 years. Yes, I still remember him!

When I see the grandchildren and observe their wit and out-going personalities, I remember my husband. He has left a part of himself behind in them. I have had the privilege of watching the grandchildren grow into such wonderful children, but I am sad that Ralph has not been alive to watch them grow up. But I hope that somehow he is looking down and knows. He would be proud! They still remember Grandpa Ralph through photos and stories; we talk about our memories of him.

If one of your loved ones has died, perhaps you too

are holding on to many precious memories of your loved one as you cautiously move on toward the future. But your loved one will always be a part of you, no matter where your new path leads. Love does not end when someone dies.

And when I see the golds, the pinks, and oranges of the sunsets splashed in splendor across the Kansas sky, I still remember my husband. I remember him saying, "*Dolly, remember me when you see the sunset,*" and I do. And many others still remember him, for he touched their lives as well. We still remember you; you have left your mark—you will not be forgotten.

*"To live in hearts we leave behind is not to die."*
—Thomas Campbell

# Sunset, Sunrise

*M*arch 2, 1962—my first date with my husband, even though I did not think it would be a date. I had gone to an evening chapel service at a college with two of my roommates, girls I rented a house with in Springfield, Missouri. After the service, Ralph, who I later married, asked me and one of my roommates to go out for pizza with him and a friend, and we went.

I never laughed so much in an evening! Having been raised in a reserved minister's family where laughter was not a regular occurrence, Ralph's fun-loving, jovial personality was refreshing! Not only did we go out March 2, but every night for the next six nights. We were married on December 28 of that year, and God blessed us with two daughters and forty-four wonderful years together.

Now fast-forward to March 2, 2006, to Ralph's respect calls at the funeral home in Miltonvale, Kansas, after his battle with kidney cancer. Many friends and family came to express their condolences, and that evening brought our life full circle from our first date on March 2, 1962, to March 2, 2006, forty-four years of sunrises and sunsets together.

Ralph and I enjoyed making pictures of sunrises and sunsets. We even kept a camera in the car to catch the colors at their peak! And on the night of March 2, 2006, according to those traveling from Clay Center, Kansas, to Miltonvale for respect calls, the sunset had been spectacular! It was as if a huge canvas of colors had been rolled out across the west-ern sky. God had outdone Himself painting a sunset with brilliant pinks, golds, and oranges, reassurance that all was well with Ralph.

But that is not "the rest of the story," as Paul Harvey would say. Now let's move forward to the wee hours of the morning of September 28, 2012—exactly six years and seven months after Ralph died. That morning I dreamed that I was again at in our old farmhouse, a place we called Thornberry Acres, where I spent many years with Ralph and our daughters.

Food was cooking on the stove—I could smell the aromas! Our kitchen and dining room were filled with family and friends, and Ralph was there. He was no longer thin and gaunt as when he died—he looked healthy! He was laughing and telling stories to those around him, just as he always did. The dining room table was fully extended with all six leaves, giving room for everyone to sit, and the table was set.

Then I woke up and realized the whole thing was a dream. I remembered that Ralph had died over six years ago, that I had sold Thornberry Acres, had married Tom, and moved into town. My life had drastically changed—the sun had set on my life with Ralph.

My huge sense of loss overwhelmed me, and tears streamed down my face. I wept for Ralph's death; I wept for Thornberry Acres—for our life in the old farmhouse. But I could not go back.

In the semi-darkness of that early dawn I saw my wonderful husband Tom quietly sleeping beside me. As I wiped away my tears, I thought of what life is like for me now. When Tom and I had married, we had doubled our children—4 now instead of 2. Grandchildren—9 instead of 4. My life had drastically changed but was good again.

Since I was scheduled to work that morning, I made

my way to the kitchen in the semi-darkness to start the coffee. That was when I noticed a glowing sunrise outside the east kitchen window, complete with amazing colors! God had again rolled out His canvas, but this time across the *eastern* sky! There were fuschias, oranges, and golds—a magnificent sight!

And then it hit me. Ralph and I had experienced our final sunset, the end of our years together, but life had gone on. I thought of the beautiful words from "Fiddler on the Roof." *"Sunrise, sunset, sunrise, sunset, swiftly fly the years. One season following another. Laden with happiness and tears."*

On that morning of September 28, 2012, I realized that I would *never* forget Ralph, no matter how many years passed by. Ralph is a part of who I am! But I realized I had moved on, reaching out for a new life, a different life.

I had said good-bye to my life with Ralph at Thornberry Acres, determined to make something good come from his death—to squeeze as much from my remaining years as possible. I thought about how the words to the song could be reversed to fit my life: "Sunset, *sunrise*, sunset, *sunrise*, swiftly fly the years, one season following the other, laden with happiness and tears." A new dawn had come, and I was thankful.

*\*Quote from "Sunrise, Sunset," lyrics by Sheldon Harnick, music by Jerry Bock, used by permission.*

*"Every sunset brings the promise*
*for a new dawn."*
—Ralph Waldo Emerson

# Epilogue—
# My Life Now

*M*y life significantly changed after my husband Ralph's death. Even though I had decided I probably would never remarry, when I went out with Tom, I changed my mind. His wife Jeniece had died seven weeks before my husband, and we had known each other for thirty-six years. He and his wife had attended our church where my husband Ralph was the pastor for nine years.

When Tom and I married, we doubled our children—from two to four, and our grand-children from four to eight. We have since gained another wonderful grandson when Tom's son remarried. Our families have blended well, and we are thankful.

Even though I am a country girl at heart, I sold my old farm house, Thornberry Acres, in the country and moved into town with Tom. The upkeep of my old farmhouse, the barn, and outbuildings would have taken much time and money, so I believe it was a wise decision at our ages.

I changed jobs, from working as the director of a program for infants and toddlers to working with hospice where I still work part-time with bereavement. In spite of the many changes, I realized that I, like Little Bear, have found my own patch of clover, and I am content.

As you move forward, you will never forget the one you loved. Even though Tom and I love each other, I will never forget Ralph, and Tom will never forget Jeniece. They are both are part of our lives, our history, our children, and our grandchildren—a part of who we were and are today.

If you have recently experienced the loss of someone dear to you, perhaps life still seems daunting and scary. Perhaps you are similar to an unborn butterfly, still snugly wrapped in your cocoon, afraid to emerge. But as your heart begins to heal, in your own time, you will be ready to wiggled out, spread your wings, and reach for a new future that is waiting.

You will know when it is time for you to push your way out of your cocoon, so you do not have to rush. Grief has its own time table, and when it is time, you will spread your wings and fly!

*"Things do not change; we change."*
—Henry David Thoreau

# No
# Road Maps

*g*rieving is hard work. There are no guidebooks, no roadmaps, for dealing with grief. Since we are unique individuals, what works for one person may not work for another. We grieve differently—at different paces, in different ways.

Immediately after a loss, it may take all of a person's energy just to get out of bed in the morning, get through the day, only to fall back into bed at night exhausted. You may experience an intense longing for the one who died as well as many unfamiliar emotions. Below are some simple, down-to-earth strategies to point you toward healing and hope.

 Adopt a "can-do" attitude. You are stronger than you might think—you can make it through grief even though it is difficult.

 The immune system may be compromised after a loss so take care of your health by scheduling a medical checkup.

 Our bodies are about 60-70 per cent water, so include plenty fluids in your diet each day.

 Even though you may not feel like eating much, choose a variety of nutritious foods including fruits and vegetables.

Exercise, such as walking, can help relieve depression and tone your body.

 Tears are healing; cry if you need to.

 Find a good friend or family member to talk to about your loss when you are feeling overwhelmed.

 Accept that grief may feel like a roller coaster with it ups and downs, hills and valleys.

 Listen to your senses and pamper yourself a bit with small comforts—with fragrances you like to smell, textures you like to feel, foods that taste good, and sounds that are pleasant.

 If you enjoy listening to music, choose music that will help lift your spirits.

 Writing about your grief experience can be healing, so keep notepads near.

 Don't isolate yourself. Stay in touch with friends and family; avoid those who drag you down.

 Consider making changes to your environment, maybe by painting or rearranging the furniture.

 Remember that laughter is good medicine—don't feel guilty for laughing or having fun.

Healing after a loss is a unique experience for each person. Don't judge your experience against someone else's.

 Give yourself permission to celebrate holidays and special days in a different way if needed.

 Take your time disposing of possessions of the one who died. If having them in sight is difficult, consider placing them in totes until a later date.

 The past cannot be changed, so if you have regrets try to forgive yourself and move on.

 Try to make something good come from your loss.

 It is possible to learn and grow personally as a result of your loss.

 If you are unable to carry on with day-to-day activities or if you have suicidal thoughts, talk to your doctor or a mental health professional—get some help!

 Remember that with the passage of time, the good days will outnumber the bad days.

 Doing something good for someone else will help you. Look into possibilities for volunteering at a church, hospital, or food bank.

Consider new possibilities, a new dream, a new purpose for your life. Take a class, start a new hobby, write your story, or make a career change.

 Even though a death can close doors, it can open new doors as well.

 ***Write a new ending to your story, and make it a good one!***

# About the Author

Dawn Rountree (Dawn's pen name) is a wife, mother, and grandmother. She grew up on a farm in Tennessee but has lived in Kansas for many years. Even as a child she enjoyed writing. When Dawn's husband Ralph died of kidney cancer, she began writing regularly to help deal with her own grief.

She later began leading a hospice bereavement group, writing articles about grief for group members. Her writing reflects her southern roots as she shares her own grief journey through personal stories and metaphor.

She is also the author of "Pathways through Grief," a series of pamphlets used by hospices, churches, and individuals to help those grieving during the first year after their loss, and writes a weekly column for her hometown newspaper.

Dawn is a registered nurse and licensed master social worker. She has worked as a nurse and social worker in a rural hospital, and is currently the Bereavement Coordinator at a local hospice.

# About the Artist

*P*ippa McNay studied graphic arts and illustration at California State University, Northridge, and Moorpark College, CA. She has enjoyed sharing her knowledge of art for over 16 years by teaching art classes for home schooled children. When she is not drawing or painting, she enjoys sculpting and pottery. She lives in Valley Center, KS.